Profit
Leadership
in Printing

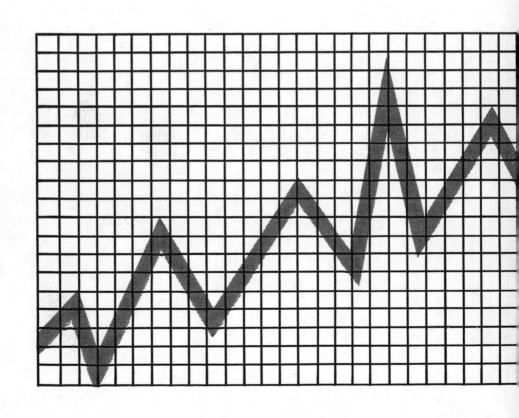

Profit Leadership in Printing

Financial Management for the Modern Printing Plant

Thomas Hughes
Economic Analyst for the Graphic Arts

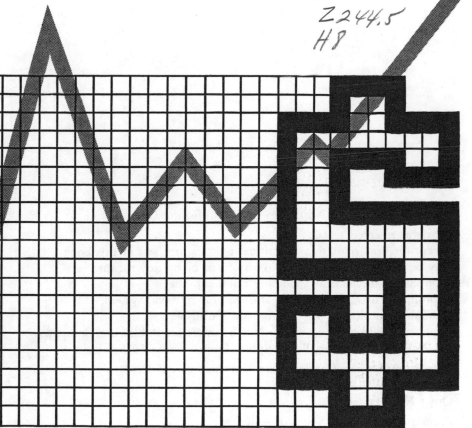

 North American Publishing Company · Philadelphia

Library of Congress Catalog Card Number: 75-28582
ISBN: 0-912920-48-3
Order Number: 125

Printed in the United States of America

Contents

Chapter 1
What Owner/Managers Must Know
About Accounting/Finance

"The growing preoccupation of managers
and management scientists with
management information systems is apparent.
In fact some see such systems
as a panacea for every type
of organizational problem."

—Russell L. Ackoff
A Concept of Corporate Planning

In the classical theories of management you'll find these listed as the major areas of authority and responsibility:

Planning;

Staffing or organizing;

Controlling.

These are the main functions of management. We are not now discussing the marketing man *vs.* the production man or line *vs.* staff.

Let's begin with a very simple definition for this over-all controlling function. Can we limit the control function to those activities designed for and implemented by management to enable it to have the corporate body conform in all operations (production–sales–administration) to pre-planned objectives, standards or goals?

If this is to be done—and it *must* be for company survival—then it is best done in an emphatic, scientific approach to the problem. There are some basic conditions or sets of general circumstances that must be present in order for this or any system of control to work:

1. There must be clearly defined goals or standards established.

2. There must be a flow of information comparing these standards to what has actually happened. This could be called "feedback."

3. When variations from standards are found, or goals are not met, corrective action must be recommended and the proper "follow-up" procedures instituted to affect this action.

If it is any consolation to the average printer trying to get some of this done for his shop, and done with very limited means usually, Item 3 is the biggest bugaboo faced by the management team at General Motors. Our small printer is in good company!

Our large over-all area of "control" breaks down into three general types:

1. The prophetic or preliminary type. This overlaps from the planning and organizing functions. This is where we do our long-term budget for capital expansion, or where we establish next year's sales goal for each salesman.

2. Current operational controls in the day-to-day paperwork of delivery slips, time sheets, job cost records and all the host of daily record-keeping tasks conforming to various and sundry minute standards, many of which are verbal and traditional in nature. This applies to all levels of management from first line foreman up to chairman of the board.

3. The final control form takes the name of Reports and Analytical Documentation of results. These are for the most part historic in nature, and may be very brief or quite detailed. There is an old rule of thumb here that the higher the level of reporting, the less details are shown. It makes sense, too! As a part of this function we must include the opinions and recommendations given for either corrective action or termination or enlargement of various segments of the business.

And then the cycle begins all over again. For it is out of last year's profit-and-loss statement that we begin with this year's budget. That is the annual cycle. Within the total system we have smaller cycles of a quarter, month, week, and even day, or shift within the day. Each has its limitations imposed by law, or traditional acceptance within the industry or firm. These traditional concepts become so strong and habit-forming that they sometimes act as blinders keeping management from advancing in areas of management progress as are other firms or other industries.

And printing is a most "traditional" business.

Now, accounting or bookkeeping is not a new tool for management. Letters of financial reporting are to be found in the tombs of the pharaohs of Egypt. We can even today examine the cost data sheet made by Anticles, the first secretary of the council of Athens. (434-433 B.C.)

Of course, some of the data are worn with time and unreadable, but the point is that even today with the ultra sophistication of computers, at the highest level this is still the basic way we compute balance of payments between the United States and France! And so what else is new?

Here in modern format is what we could observe of that year's building cost the Parthenon . . .

Balance from preceeding year XXXXXXX
Income from the treasury of goddess XXXX
From the sale of gold XXXXX
From the sale of silver XXXX
Expenditures:
Purchases . . . . . _____
Payment under contracts . . . . . _____
Quarrymen (wages) XXXX
Sculptors (wages) XXXXX
Employees paid by the month . . . . . _____
Balance remaining from this year . . . . . _____

If you are a real history buff on accounting you may review the then "new" system for double entry as devised by Luca Pacioli who wrote something that sounds like "Summa Ancient Double Entry Bookkeeping" except the words include arithmetic and geometry of all things, and don't forget "ratios." There's even a full set of documented accounting records from a merchant-banker of Avignon of 1390 that include branch accounting and the elements of corporate consolidations! Over 500 years old!

Then as now, someone was watching the bucks. Someone had the responsibility of answering to the "old man" what the bank balance was or where such and such was kept and how much was on hand or available for production.

There really isn't a lot of difference between the inventory listing of goodies to go with the pharaoh on his last voyage to the "land beyond" than there is to the inventory of X color cans of ink or skids of paper. Each serves some purpose so that someone in authority can know and can control.

In principle, the system hasn't changed too much. What has changed is how we put it all together. No longer is it a series of scribes and clerks each setting down in painful script the journal of the events of today. It is now the electronic impulse from the ringing up of a cash register, or the plastic card number that triggers a computer to give out with an estimate of cost determined for X product and by Y salesman, often several hundred miles away from either place of business or the safety lock box of the numbers—the modern computer.

How Can I Use Thee . . . Let Me Count the Ways

I Prophetic

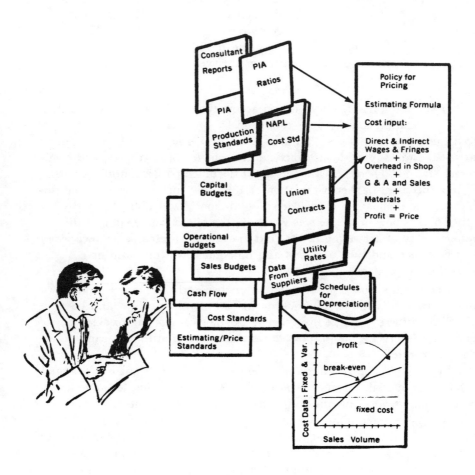

2 Now   *3* Reports

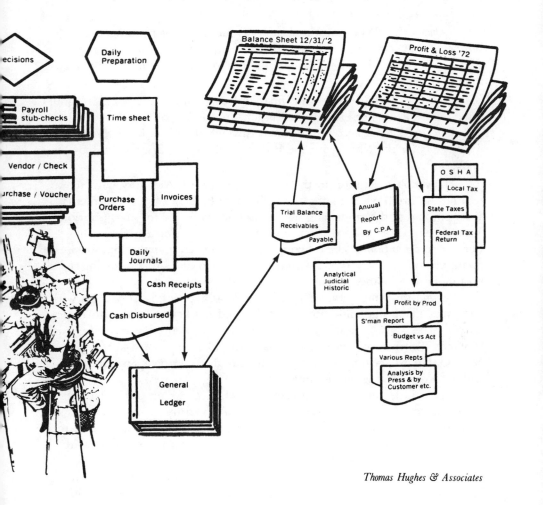

Thomas Hughes & Associates

Unanimity among accountants is found just about six feet beyond the pot of gold at the end of the rainbow. It does not exist in either classification of accounts nor in their definitions. The final format of the balance sheet, for example, can throw a group of CPA's into a tizzy. As in most cases, rank has its privileges, which means the rankest one has his way! But even then it is, first and last, both an art and a science.

In a broader sense accounting is a catalyst that brings together economics and administration into systematic methodology. Out of this mass of modern data we seek the answer to *two questions* that since the dawn of time have had management on the ropes:

Question 1: "What are the results of our efforts of running this business (or agency or government or what have you) during the past _____? You fill in the blank with the appropriate time factor: day—month—year."

Question 2: "What is our total financial position at _____ (again some point in time) or exactly how much are we worth?"

The professional accountant down through the years has standardized his answers for the No. 1 with the P & L and for No. 2 with the balance sheet.

Too simple a solution to the problem, you say? Well stay with me a minute. An inventory listing, x value, is to be found in both documents. Is its purpose to determine ending balance for value or for consumption? Value goes on the balance sheet, use or consumption on the P & L. Further combination of these two documents means that the long-term accumulation of many P & L's find their way to one single spot for reporting on the balance sheet.

Beyond this simplicity, we find today that accounting is tied up with basic manufacturing, and with both sales and marketing, and with basic economic decisions that affect every and all parts of the business. Try to convince IRS that you have done away with all your record-keeping! Even OSHA has begun to exert pressure on all record keepers. And it will get worse, not better, as time goes by.

It is a little bit like the steering wheel of a car or truck. Not too big when compared to the engine or wheels, not too costly an item when compared to the body or truck bed. Not nearly as pretty as a good paint job . . . but just try to drive without it! No industry can get along without an accounting department.

The whole field is divided between private and public accountants. We'll cover these in a later chapter. Both are professionals, one limiting his services to one firm while the other serves many. Within this first group there is the bookkeeper, the junior and senior accountants, the tax accountant, the cost accountant, the auditor, the controller, or comptroller, and the treasurer. Each is a specialist in his own way.

We have neither time nor space to devote to the problem of accounting principles (even the national CPA associations haven't solved that one yet), nor to terminology, nor even to all the basic concepts. We would like to get into an over-view of the whole system as seen through the eye of a systems chartist with a little imagination.

The big, *big* thing to remember about this servant of management is that it surrounds and engulfs him at all times; therefore he better make an all-out effort to speak the language of general finance, for he cannot survive long without it.

Chapter 2
"Number Dummies" or
Profit Police?

"When constabulary duty's to be done,
a policeman's lot is not a happy one."
—William S. Gilbert

This all-powerful man who "runs the numbers"—is he court jester and fool or is he the keeper of the keys and seal with all the power of the Chancellor of the Exchequer? Shakespeare had him called a "fool who keeps the purse." A bit far fetched as far as today goes, except when a craftsman-operator-owner tries to be all things to himself and run the numbers untrained.

The man who controls the money of a firm and does the financial management often wears more than one hat. In very large firms the hats are designed and suited to specialties and several men wear them. To prove a point, for just two days we examined the *Wall Street Journal* for ads seeking men of this type. The ever-expanding marketplace of American business sets the standards and often defines the job, regardless of what the so-called professional or scholar thinks of his title or degree. Here are typical ads:

"Vice President Finance: Qualifications: Must have extensive experience in Controllership, procedures and budgeting and controls, cash management, consolidations and financial reporting."

"Financial Management Executives: Create Your Own Position: . . . Experience in financial management . . . could be as controller, financial analyst, accounting manager . . . must be aggressive, well organized, articulate and able to manage people . . . able to plan, analyze and implement major programs leading to sound financial management . . . personal ambition and aggressiveness are paramount."

Now let's examine what they are looking for in controllers:

"Controller reporting directly to the President . . . background in standard cost accounting, profit planning, computer management and credit management.

"To assume the responsibilities of controller . . . all facets of general accounting, budgeting, cash planning, taxes and (government) reporting."

Another like entry added EDP and systems and procedures to the list of duties. A third, with its list, added still other duties including "banking relations, cash flow, personnel functions such as benefit programs, salary administration, employee selection, contracts and coordination of projects."

For the assistant controller or, as one ad stated, comptroller, they listed these duties: "accounting policies and practices, guidance to decentralized subsidiaries, accounting, control and management information systems (plans) . . . setting and achieving targets . . . reports to vice president and controller."

Incidental to our survey, this last firm is an old friend. We worked on its audit some 25 years ago and almost took that same job with it when it was an unlisted firm.

Added to our list of financial men must be the old breed called the auditor, or a more fancy term today, internal auditor or director of internal audits. Their job requirements include: design of internal audit programs, procedures for cash controls, selection of accounting personnel and staff training. Some ads spell out such things as "prefer 'big 8' experience at the senior level and CPA status."

Now move forward into the new breed of financial men, who wear titles like: vice president of systems and data processing; management, EDP systems; or corporate data processing consultant. All have new and very specific duties relative to number controls, and processing and reporting with corporate bodies.

The new breed doesn't stop with computers. But what goes on after the printouts are delivered to the executive suites? Here's a quick rundown on these new jobs:

"Director of Financial Analysis: experience of three years in financial management as a line controller, or planning manager. Responsibilities include: capital (budget) . . . review of profit plan, analysis of variances, development of long range plans, deal with all operating key management . . . and interface with key corporate personnel."

Financial Innovator . . . through understanding of the corporate financial function . . . Familiarity with applied computer technology is essential as well as the ability to interact with senior management."

Such terms as corporate financial planning and analysis specialist, or manager of financial analysis are not new to the world of finance any more. They are as common as last month's newspaper—which is where they all come from!

9

The computer hasn't put accountants out of work, it has created hundreds of new tasks that need human judgment after the race is run and the final tally is in.

Questions of how to run the race next time must be answered. The men who analyze finances help management decide that one.

The point we are trying to make is that this breed of professional people, old or new, *are whatever the job calls for.* This kind of individual is sought after at all levels of corporate growth. At the beginning, perhaps, *one man has to do it all.* He is usually a busy, harassed man. If the owner tries to do it himself, plus run the shop in both production and sales, something has to give. *And it usually is the financial control.*

Years ago I remember reading where Dun & Bradstreet had listed causes for failure. Up near the top of the list was lack of business experience and improper financial controls.

In our industry most of the small shops and the medium-size ones are run by *excellent craftsmen.* Years of working experience with presses, plates and type attest to their ability. But with the balance sheet, profit-and-loss statement, or cash flow, some are babes in the woods. They don't hear howling off in the distance.

A rundown of the specific duties, in brief, for the money men—"the number dummies" among us—would read something like this:

The Treasurer: (1) Files reports of financial condition and all tax reports; (2) stockholder or owner reports; (3) custody of cash, funds, securities; (4) all bank transactions; (5) keeps books of account, cash journals, and (6) advises the corporation on financial matters.

Another half-dozen or so could be added, all a further, finite part of each of these major items.

The Controller: (1) Principal accounting officer in charge of accounting books and records (conflict with no. 5 for treasurer); (2) audits payroll and vouchers; (3) plans, establishes and issues standard practices for all accounting matters, and coordinates the system throughout the whole organization; (4) maintains and enforces rules regarding reports, and/or compliance with governmental bodies; (5) files required reports and statistics; (6) prepares balance sheets, and profit-and-loss statements, income accounts, and all financial reports and statements, plus the budget; (7) makes payments, issues checks, vouchers, drafts, etc., and (8) handles leases, insurance, dividends, tax matters, etc.

And we now begin to see how *these functions overlap.* We have at this point only taken two of the many titles to define. Some have prepared comparative task listings for these and other corporate officers, such as the secretary, and find that many of these tasks are *divided by tradition* within the individual firm. Many are performing a certain function today because a previous man sitting in their chair assumed that task several decades ago.

What's all this got to do with printing?

Well now, if financial management is necessary to business growth and development in other industries, isn't it a matter of logic that printers need it too? But aren't most of us far, far and away too small to *acquire such high priced men.*

That's where we might well differ in opinion.

Many of our owners in printing don't own a typesetter. They buy type on the outside. It is a necessary part of the cost of doing the job for the customer.

Why not have this kind of work done that way also? It makes a lot of sense.

We took the ads listed in the April 1973 issue of *Printing Impressions* and reviewed them for these job types. We've included a run-down of what we found in the table above. Please note that out of 146 job openings *only six* were in the upper levels of management, and *only two of those were for financial men!*

Could it be that this is the major cause of such a low national profit level? We can sell, we can print, we can design artwork, bind books and set type, *but do we make enough money* for this total output effort?

I don't think we do. And a major cause is the almost total lack of competent financial management in the small and medium-size shop.

Now don't get me wrong—everyone isn't in that category. The small, well-managed shop owner does well. Very well! He sells and produces at a profit margin many times over what the average man gets for the same or like effort.

For example: Out of the absolute data section of the '73 PIA ratios these figures come up for our review. The real dollars of profit by leaders differ from the "also ran" group as follows:

	Additional $	
Very small size: under		
$250,000	$19,490	Profit
Small: $250,000/		
$500,000	29,600	
Medium: $500,000/		
$1,500,000	82,840	
Medium: $1,500,000/		
$5,000,000	216,860	
Large: $5,000,000/		
$10,000,000	681,400	

Remember, *that's not the profit made by the leader group,* but the
ADDITIONAL PROFIT he made over his average, lower-money-making
peer group. The difference comes from the six M's and a C: Men,
Materials, Machines, Motivation, Money and Methods—all run by
CONTROL.

Those who have control of what it's all about laugh all the way to
the bank. Those who do not usually have more sales, and less profit dollars.
More headaches, and more paper to buy, more customer problems, more this
and more that—everthing, except where the score counts. The bottom line of
the P & L shows less for the efforts put forth than the well-managed firm
that controls.

If you can't find the time to do this control job, hire it done. Get
your CPA and his staff to give you some time. It will be money well
spent. It will return seven-fold to the coffers. Don't knock this until
you've tried it. Every firm that I have seen take this route in the past six
years—and it's the gospel we preach to small management—has improved
its profit picture considerably.

And we are not just alluding to the very small. One web house has
turned over some of this financial management analysis work and
budgetary tasks to its CPA, being already aware of money leaks in the
shop. They'll be plugged this year for more profits next year. It makes sense.
It also makes cents and dollars, believe me.

Help Wanted Ads in Printing Impressions, April 1973

Total Jobs Analyzed	General Job Description	$10,000 to 12,000	$12,000 to 15,000	$15,000 to 20,000	$20,000 to 25,000	$25,000 to 30,000	$30,000 to 40,000	Over $40,000
6	General management, administration finance. vice presidential levels manufacturing			1	1	1	1	2
26	Marketing & sales management	1	4	5	5	6	3	2
30	Salesmen & sales reps.	6	6	9	4	3	2	
38	Plant supervision, shift superintendents, production control		2	9	19	7	1	
2	Industrial relations			1	1			
10	Estimator	3	3	3	1			
	Department general foremen:							
13	Pressroom	1	4	5	3			
2	Composition					2		
7	Platemaking	2	1	3	1			
12	Bindery	4	4	1	3			
146	Totals	19	31	47	26	13	6	4

Chapter 3
The Quality of
Leadership Among Us

"The genius of a good leader
is to leave behind him
a situation which common sense,
without the grace of genius,
can deal with successfully."

—Walter Lippmann

Just about one out of every five company presidents is a real leader.
With that single statement I have made more enemies than I can possibly
dodge the remaining few years of life! This not-so-casual observation is
made after looking at all industry from within and without this past 30
years. And, hard as this statement is, it is more than likely very true. Nor
is it limited to our industry only.

If we cross over into the field of politics perhaps the rate goes so
very low we'd be forced to use decimal points! But politics is not our
beat, so to speak. Leadership, pure and simple, is first of all almost
always not so very pure and far from simple. Our desire to over-simplify
things just makes it seem that way.

Our Exhibit 1 shows the financial results of almost 1,000 firms in our
printing industry—what they did in 1973 as reported in the 1974 PIA
Ratio Studies, for both general printers and for the trade shops serving
them. Not all of them, of course, just those who entered into this finest
of management financial surveys, this prime tool for increased profitability. One out of five is a profit leader.

We've taken the raw data as contained on the absolute data pages of
these various studies and refined them a bit into their parts of profit
leaders and others. We've averaged out the two sections and we are in a
position to be objective as to their differences.

The first thing we notice is the almost perfect 20/80 division between
leaders and followers in the race for profit dollars. The 20/80 limitation
by *Economic Law* prevails in all sections of our business. Among printers it

is 20.7 to 79.3; with typesetters it is 18 to 82; among platemakers is is 19 to 81, and with bindery owners it is 17 to 83. Overall it is 20.4 to 79.6 . . . about as close to 20/80 as one could get! Or, with the money-makers, it is four to one, or *one out of five!*

Our use of this data is subject to some very minor deviation, which we have shown in a footnote to the exhibit. But for this general purpose, it is close enough.

However, since we are forever examining leadership in the light of who made what, there is a danger that we may overlook the qualities of managership that brought them to that place in the beginning. Before we get into the philosophy of management and leadership in general, perhaps a second exhibit is in order. Our Exhibit 2 is a regional trade association of almost one-quarter of a hundred firms that entered the 1974 Ratios, so these firms are buried within the total data of Exhibit 1.

What we've done is taken a very hypothetical situation and plotted these firms out on a graph as they might normally appear, had we each and every firms' P & L to examine, which neither we nor anyone else can ever do. The data are as close kept a secret as the combination to the gold vault at Fort Knox, so our bell curve is *guesswork*. The only thing we know is that, most likely, the regional will closely follow the pattern of the whole group. Just in the same manner that the trade shops follow the printer.

Among 24 firms, you'd be likely to find about five above 8% net, and the remaining 19 scattered down from 6 or 7% to a 1% level. Take this bell curve and multiply by 40, fill in some of the missing spaces and you'd have a picture of what Exhibit 1 shows, in slightly different format. The story would be the same, the characters would not have changed, nor the plot either for that matter.

And what a plot it is. A story in four parts. In part one, our other typesetters could be making an additional $62,400 on their same volume of business . . . if they were of the leadership. The difference is even greater among the platemakers. If the volume of sales stayed the same but the profit principles were applied all year long, it would mean an additional $86,700 at year-end. The differences among binders is almost a case of truth stranger than fiction! The binders come up some $167,800 short of the profit leaders. After seeing the profit differential, examine the sales differential also. This is a real case of the joys of good managers.

Among printers, the same size business should have produced an added $175,000 to the profit kitty.

Every time we mention this we hear such comments as: "Well, they just don't have our problems." True, true, true. They either had a problem prevention system working or solved them with far less effort and time loss.

The bindery situation is a case in point. On sales far, far under the others, these profit leaders made much more money for the stockholders. Could it be that they had dumped the unprofitable business? I know this happened with one owner. He lost a good chunk of business, and along with it a far greater portion of his overall management problems. What was left gave him a greater year-end profit than previous years, with 30% less sales. This guy is now a believer in not only being selective in empoyees and equipment, but even more so he is *selective in sales*. He prices right and will *not* take the no-profit job!

This morning the phone rang. A midwest printer wanted some work done. He had been a 14% leader among his peer group, but last year was different—new plant to move into, changes within the management team, and then came the economic/oil/energy problem. Wage/cost/price/pull or what have you . . . it wasn't a good year. His 1974 P & L reflects that he is still in the leader group at better than 8%, but what is unique is that, in addition to the present pressure of a wild economy, he is planning expansion.

New presses and new bindery equipment are on order. Delivery will be in the late '75 and early '76. Could we run a projected budget, hourly-cost rates, recalculate *overhead absorption* after the addition of the new capital items, calculate break-even points for one- and two-shift work, and do some return on investment calculations? What's the point of this? He is a leader. He knows just *exactly* where he is going, and *how* he'll get there. Economic recession or not, he is among the leaders in good times as well as bad. Almost all the others of like cut-of-cloth *stay up there among the winners.*

Now comes the question: How do they do it?

These men put their pants on each morning as we all do—one leg at a time. What makes them different at year-end when the bottom lines of the P & L separate the leaders from all us others?

Answers to these questions cannot be finite like X dollars of bad debts or X percentage of ink usage. Oh, no . . . now we move over in philosophy and mind-bending with a slight touch of Lady Luck.

We know that Solomon, the wisest of them all, said: "The race is not to the swift, nor the battle to the strong, neither yet bread to the wise, nor yet riches to men of understanding, nor yet favor to men of skill; but time and chance happeneth to them all." The very term "fortune" has come to mean wealth as well as luck. Our concern is not with it, but what basic principles will help the odds in our fight for corporate survival and profit leadership.

If we had to name some real simple *common sense* words of what these leaders have, it might be these:

Fortitude—this has to come first! Not because I say so, but because I believe one of the outstanding men of this century, Winston Churchill, placed this quality first among leaders. In common language it is called *guts*, the quality that resists, endures and triumphs over all the trials and temptations of life.

Since the term "prude" has taken on such a distasteful connotation, I almost hesisitate to use an old-fashioned word like "prudence," but *prudence* is another quality I see in most leaders. The ability to govern and discipline self by the use of logical reason—this is prudence! Without it, where would we be with respect to wisdom, impartiality or even such a little thing as tact?

There seems to be one quality sorely missing from life today—justice. Giving everyone his just due is the bedrock of honesty. This precept could even be applied to politics!

If the stool of leadership has four legs, the fourth one just might be *temperance*. Self-control and moderation is the highest development of man in the natural state. It serves both our social and business life well.

Don't look upon such terms as *"humility"* as being a sign of weakness. It is not. It is the signature of greatness. When putting together his auto-biography in 1771, our old Philadelphia Printer added up some 13 virtues and their precepts, and closed with the comment: "#13 Humility. Imitate Jesus and Socrates."

Now be honest. If some bright lad said that to your personnel manager, what kind of reception would the comment receive? Haven't we left those common old virtues behind for the adult level sophistry of the 19th hole business meeting and the wisdom gained from a lunch of four martinis or scotch and waters? By coincidence, a recent issue of the *Wall Street Journal* had a lead story with the headline: "Booze Business, Liquor and Corruption are Drinking Buddies."

We really didn't intend to get into this matter, but more than a little fuzzy management thinking comes from too much bottle. We once had a boss who always refused the second lunch drink with a client firm.

He had a standard answer: "If I take another, I may make promises the firm can't keep."

Now just what is this leadership business anyway? It is a broad subject, encompassing education, the military establishment, civil and social life as well as business. Our concern is with the last-named only. We have done a bit of research on what some of the great leaders of this present age think of the subject. They range from a five-star general to an inventor and space explorer. Here's what these national leaders think of their own peer group:

Leadership is, at the beginning, a fight for the control of the hearts and minds of men.

Leadership is at first intellectual. Maybe this definition will do. It is the *capacity* and the *will* to rally men and women to a common purpose. *Leadership* is having the capacity plus the *will* to use it!

Leadership is built on a base of truth and character. A leader is the servant of truth. That truth is the focus of a common purpose. He must have the force of a strong character necessary to inspire others to follow him with confidence. Call it will power.

What is "character"? Let's define it as (1) knowing what you want to do and (2) having the determination to do it. And in a way which will inspire confidence in those for whom you are responsible. You lead; they follow:

The leader must have *infectious optimism,* and the *absolute determination* to persevere in the face of any and all difficulties. He must also radiate confidence, relying on both moral and spiritual principles. He must use all resources to work out a right solution even when he himself is not too certain of the material outcome. He must have a sound judgment in which others will have confidence, and a firm knowledge of human nature. He must be able to see his problems objectively and in whole. *Self-control* is an absolute component of his make-up.

That's quite a man!

Leadership is being a good selector of men, the ability to pick good subordinates. Once having selected them, the leader must know how to train them!

Some people think that pre-eminence in a sport is necessary in order to be a leader. It may help in developing leadership but is in no way a necessity. There is no need to be a gladiator in sport to be a leader, nor a killer to be a general.

The true leader must be able to dominate, and finally to master, all the events which surround him. He must never let events get the better of him. If he does, he will lose confidence and will cease to be of any value as a leader.

One final test of a leader is the feeling you have when you leave his presence after a conference or interview. Have you a feeling of uplift and confidence? Are you clear as to what is to be done, and what your part of the task is? Are you determined to pull your weight in achieving the object? Or is your feeling the reverse?

In Machiavelli's *The Prince*, we read: "To exercise the intellect a man should read histories, and study there the actions of illustrious men, to see how they have borne themselves in war, to examine the causes of their victories and defeat."

Perhaps because we honor Ole Ben Franklin during Printing Week each January, we should take time just to read his list of virtues: 1. Temperance; 2. Silence; 3. Order; 4. Resolution; 5. Frugality; 6. Industry; 7. Sincerity; 8. Justice; 9. Moderation; 10. Cleanliness; 11. Tranquility; 12. Chastity; 13. Humility.

They wouldn't make much of a TV series for us sophisticates today, would they? But most leaders I know in printing wear that cut of cloth.

Exhibit 1

1974 Profit Leadership in the Graphic Arts Industry

Profit Leader Group (top quintile)

		Average Assets	Sales	Net Profits	Percent
7	Typesetters	$ 518,900	$1,103,400	$114,700	10.40%
7	Platemakers	2,377,400	4,121,300	404,300	9.81%
6	Binders	394,000	702,700	93,700	13.34%
183	Printers	1,475,400	2,547,000	282,500	11.08%
203	Total Group	$1,440,500	$2,200,700	$275,300	11.88%

Comparative Peer Group (lower four quintiles)

32	Typesetters	$ 414,300	$ 811,300	$22,000	2.71%
29	Platemakers	634,000	1,459,700	56,500	3.87%
30	Binders	791,400	1,753,200	66,100	3.77%
698	Printers	1,261,500	2,228,200	71,600	3.21%
789	Total Group	$1,186,200	$2,170,800	$68,900	3.17%

Source: Absolute Data Sections of all major PIA Ratio Studies for the four classifications listed. *1974.* All rounded off to nearest $100.00. Margin of error (in deviation) from detailed Operating Statements: Total groups were 2/100 of one percent; profit leaders were 14/100 of one percent due to smaller data base. Profit Leader group, in total, 203 out of combined 992 firms equals an almost perfect 20% or upper quintile. Once again the law of 20/80 at work in our industry.

Exhibit 2

Regional Distribution of *Profit Leaders* and other firms
According to Net Profit from Operations
Five above 8% = Profit Leaders
Nineteen under 8% = Others or 'Also Ran'

Number of Firms

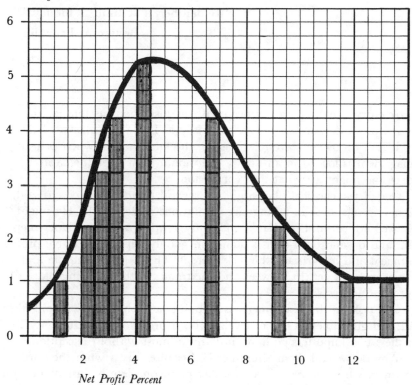

Net Profit Percent

Statistical Probabilities with this number
(following the larger national pattern)

One firm at 1 to 2%
Two firms at 2 to 3%
Three firms at about 3%
Four firms at about 3.5%
Five firms at about 4.3%
Four firms at about 6.5%
Five firms above 8%

Chapter 4
Profit Control
Rules of Thumb

"Remember that time is money."
—Benjamin Franklin

Double-entry bookkeeping has been with us just about as long as the printing press, the former, in the last analysis, being the master of the two. It isn't an owner-slave relationship, though at times when printing management is locked in an intense emotional fight over the capital budget one might arrive at that conclusion.

One of the classical playwrights of several hundred years ago said: "Money speaks sense in a language all nations understand." He might have well added: and my banker, and my supplier and my paper merchant and on and on. Profit is money in goodly supply, excessive profits too much, and bankruptcy the lack thereof. That's just as simple and basic as one can get. In between these extremes is the dwelling place of most printing firms.

Our task, in this assignment, is to point out some pitfalls along the road, and guidelines to higher levels of both profit and productivity. For these two imposters go hand in hand, almost without exception.

Why do we call them "imposters"? Because this is what they are sometimes, when the records are inexact or incomplete or just plain "not there." Things have a way of being very deceptive without the proper controls, methods, procedures and basic principles. It is bad enough and inexact enough when all is going well in accounting. As a profession in the management sciences, some classify it just above witchcraft. Or is it below? Anyway, to many men on the management team words like "budget" or "standard" or "variance" cause the heart to beat faster, sweat to appear on the brow and the mouth to run dry.

Many men can master bowling averages, batting averages and golf scores and yet they do an absolute flip when confronted with ratios of operations at the plant or department level. These are just basic tools of management that count up the hits, runs and errors of business. It is the scorecard of passes completed or putts that were sunk. Nothing more, nothing less.

The most important scorecard you will keep as a top level executive is the operating statement, or what most people in the business field call the P & L. This single one-page document recaps in cogent format the most revealing historic data of the most recent accounting period of the firm.

In final format, each is the design of the particular executive who makes use of it. Some like an accounting for operations without comparisons, some with a budget comparison, some with the same period of the previous year . . . and on and on. Our Exhibit 1 shows a normal operating statement for an average printer who participated in both the 1972 and 1971 PIA ratio studies. This is data from those years but reported (and dated by the report) as 1973 and 1972 respectively.

We've added a third column for dollar variances. Some do and some don't—each, as we said, designed with a set of particulars and prejudices in mind. When we get into the P & L report in greater detail we'll try to present a standardized format that gives both current period (month) and year to date, with comparisons to previous year and budget. All possible for presentation on one 8½x11" sheet.

Yet this one document tells the story of success or failure in the market place—and also in the production areas, as well as showing where the fat is in both administrative and sales departments. Well worth knowing and heeding? You bet your money it is!

Taking our Exhibit 1, let's make use of the various major ratios that we can tag as basic rules of thumb for printers. First the *Operating Profit Percentage*. This is:

$$\frac{D}{A} \quad or \quad \frac{the\ Gross\ or\ Operating\ Profit}{Net\ Sales}$$

In this case it is: $\dfrac{\$\ 385,600}{2,000,000}$

. . . or 19.28 percent for 1972.

A good rule of thumb is to keep this ratio at or about the 20-percent level. This past year the profit leader firms stood at the 23.89-percent mark.

Our second basic rule of thumb should be our *Net Profit Ratio.*

This is: $\dfrac{E}{A}$ or $\dfrac{96,400}{2,000,000}$

. . . or 4.82 percent.

Every firm has its own set of goals—here we should try to keep it at the 6-percent level *at least.* Otherwise invest your money in E bonds— you'll sleep better at night and not risk cardiac arrest!

Of course the profit leader firms *all* average better than 8 percent net. In fact, last year they were running at almost 11 percent; 10.99 percent, to be accurate!

My third and fourth rules are two sides of the same coin. It is the measurement of payrolls in production areas to the value added by manufacturing. PIA (Printing Industries of America) has called this "inside sales" since the 1969 PIA national convention, getting it from a national public accounting firm. Personally I think the term not too accurate as a description of what "value added" really is. Just for once we'll stick with the governmental agencies as being better than the professions.

Value added is nothing more to the printer than converting the ink in cans to ink on the paper. It is what takes place in the integrated manufacturing process known as printing. It begins with art and design, composition is an early step, lead or camera plates that serve the same end purpose get the job part way completed, binders and finishers do just that. The net additional worth of the conversion process is our value added or inside sales.

The formula here is: $\dfrac{C}{A-B}$ or $\dfrac{\text{Factory Payrolls}}{\text{Net Sales - Total Materials}}$

in this case it is: $\dfrac{683,800}{2,000,000 - 706,400}$

. . . or 52.86 percent.

Our rule of thumb should be at or about the 50-percent level. With our profit leaders last year it was 48.01 percent.

Now for my favorite (here we show our prejudices and educational background brainwashings). If you take the reverse tack for the formula above you have: $\dfrac{A-B}{C}$

. . . or perhaps the most significant long-term factor in our industry. (See Exhibit 2 for the past ten-year cycle and trend line. More on that later.)

This may be termed the economics of productivity. It is a true economic measurement of just what you get in *production value per $1.00 of labor input.* The long-term rule of thumb should be $2.00 even.

For this last actual case it becomes:

$$\frac{\$2,000,000 - 706,400}{683,800}$$

. . . or $1.89.

That sure is a miserable figure for our industry. Exhibit 2 will show you why.

Rules of thumb aside, permit us a comment or two on two items that need to be understood by printing management. First is that these ratios, as derived from PIA or NAPL, are perfectly valid. The industry has in the PIA standards probably the finest set of base data available to any industry in the world today. It has been a model of the total accounting profession since the mid 1920's. The accounting handbook series has used the PIA figures as examples of excellence in the management tools area.

The second need for printing management to recognize is the overall sickness of our industry. In Exhibit 2, take care to note our long-term (ten-year) trend line on the strong downside (now we speak with forked tongue of securities analyst) going from bad to even worse in this productivity business. Why more and more regional managers in trade association work don't make use of such data for negotiations is beyond me.

We just threw in the 1928 figure to show the great long, long-term validity of the data base. While a number of printers fail to recognize these as management tools, those who do profit from it quite well.

As the eternal rule of 80/20 goes—with 80 percent of the profits being made by 20 percent of the printers—so it is that the 20 percent are the users of each and every tool available.

Accounting isn't what it used to be. Go check out a current college catalog and you'll see what we mean. Students now in school working for an MBA with a major in accounting become quite conversant with such items as computer concepts, direct costing and contribution accounting. Add to that such items as flexible budgeting, performance reporting, economic evaluation of capital expenditures, and now even into the arena with "behavioral science implications for management accounting." It has gone as far beyond bookkeeping as a Harris M-1000 is beyond a platen press.

We'd like to continue our investigation into the management profit and control field with a chapter devoted to such items as the basic principles behind corporate accounting, a look-see at what some people call the number dummy. You may call him a controller or a comptroller or treasurer or even an accountant. What is he, what does he do? From here we'll move into an examination of your balance sheet and into more details on the operating statement. Then we'll get into some other goodies too. We'll even be brave enough to look at budgeted hourly costs and try a do-it-yourself session on individual cost centers: how to set them up and keep them current.

In 1747, Old Ben, the then printer, said . . . "Many have been ruined by buying good penny-worths." If that's applicable to your attitude towards your own financial record keeping, take a warning word. Change, and for the better. Spend a buck or two toward improvement. It'll pay off in the best way possible. Don't put it off.

Exhibit 1

Comparative Operating Report: Mr. Average Printer USA

		1972	1971	*Variances* *'72 over (under)*
A	Sales Value of Production	$2,000,000	$2,000,000	
	Materials: Paper	436,400	417,800	18,600
	Outside Services & Other	270,000	277,800	(7,800)
B	Total Materials	706,400	695,600	10,800
C	Factory Payrolls	683,800	680,600	3,200
	Factory Expenses:			
	Fixed	112,600	114,400	(1,800)
	Variable	111,600	108,600	3,000
	Total Factory Expenses	224,200	223,000	1,200
	Total Factory Cost	1,614,400	1,599,200	15,200
D	Gross Profit	385,600	400,800	(15,200)
	Administrative Cost	140,400	145,400	(5,000)
	Selling Expenses	141,000	157,600	(16,600)
	Total G & A and Sales Cost	281,400	303,000	(21,600)
	Operating Profit	104,200	97,800	6,400
	Other Income & Expenses	(7,800)	(11,000)	3,200
E	Net Profit	$ 96,400	$ 86,800	$ 9,600

Exhibit 2

Sales Value of Production per $1.00 of Labor Input

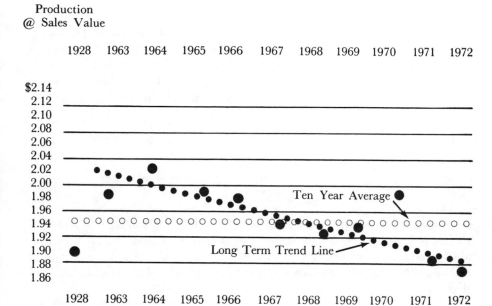

Source: PIA Ratio Studies, years indicated.

Chapter 5
Don't Ignore the
Balance Sheet

"The financial statement
may reflect a company's past,
but how much does it tell of the future—
or of the men whose actions today,
determine tomorrow's profits?"

—Clarence B. Randall
The Myth of the Perfect Balance Sheet

Aristotle gave his views on the achievement of our goals in life—such as success and happiness—when he stated: "First have a definite, clear, practical ideal—a goal, an objective. Second, have the necessary means to achieve your end—wisdom, money, materials and methods. Third, adjust your means to that end."

Sounds like something from George Dively at a Printing Industries of America (PIA) management seminar.

The prime function of the basic management documents that measure these four parts of the "means to the end"—the balance sheet and the operating statement—is to tell it like it is. Or, as in the case of the operating statement, to tell it like it was. What our old Greek friend had to say may well be better classified under general business philosophy than accounting. It does, nevertheless, fit the current, more materialistic economic viewpoints of this and the last century.

With all due apologies to the various Watergate witnesses, we have to deal with "some point in time" when we speak of the balance sheet. For the date of the document is the first item of the reported data. It spells out the financial condition of a firm as of a particular day, at the close of business therein. It is very specific and absolute.

A rose by any other name would still be a balance sheet, even when it's called a statement of financial condition, or statement of assets and liabilities,

26

or we may even add "and net worth," to the last set of descriptives. How about statement of ownership, or statement of affairs? You name it! Others have and they have been accepted during varying time and for sundry reasons.

Some have added such descriptive terms as "condensed," or "comparative" or "consolidated" or "proforma," each having some special meaning to the accountants charged with preparing the document as well as the management group it has been prepared for. Some are made up of summary figures, brief and concise. Some are of two different periods of time for the same firm, some include the reports of minor firms partly owned by the company making the report.

Views of balance sheets differ in great degrees. What is the role of the viewer? Is he a banker making a short-term loan? Is he an underwriter providing funds for the long term? Does he seek to buy the firm? Or is he seeking a normal credit reference check? Each man will view from a different angle.

We'll spend our time in this little effort viewing it as a member of a management team engaged in the search for a better more profitable tomorrow. How do we get it? What will the balance sheet tell us?

During the course of operation of any business there comes the time when the owners need to know just where they stand as to what they own, what is due them from others, and what they owe others. The balance sheet answers three questions. In the text *Practical Controllership*** it is stated: "Structurally, though of course *not in management importance,* the balance sheet is the basic financial statement, and all others are supplementary to it, or derive from it."

This role of being the basic document is often overlooked by most management because of the *importance* factor. The operating statement usually gets the most attention. It tells us what we did, not where we are. There is one section of the balance sheet though, that will tell us the "what we did" in very clipped, precise terms; not only for the most recent period, but also how we have done over the life of the firm. (More on that later.)

This summary format of the operating statement, often buried in the depths of the balance sheet offers proof for the authors above. Despite

---

* 3rd Ed., David R. Anderson et al., Richard D. Irwin, Inc., Homewood, Ill., 1973.

this, we must recognize the subservient role played by the balance sheet in most management circles.

For a clear and concise understanding of any corporate or partnership effort, both basic financial reports are an absolute necessity.

Just what does the usual balance sheet show? To begin with there is no more a "usual" balance sheet than there is an "average firm." Both are figments of imagination in the terminology of writers, teachers and statisticians, But they do have a place in explicables, such as this present effort. We'd be lost without the ability to turn to averages for "examples." And in that regard we've prepared Exhibit 1 of a series of averages for medium-size printers who took part in the 1973 PIA Ratio Study.. The first column is the profile or average of the 45 profit leader firms and the second column that of the others who "also ran."

We have used this particular size group because it should be the most relevant to the greatest number of readers. This is the group with sales between $500,000 and $1.5 million per year. In fact, these two groups have almost identical sales: $917,000 for the profit leaders and $918,800 for the others. Beyond that point the similarities disappear.

You will note that there are half a dozen key sections or classifications in this report, and it is patterned after the standard form of reporting the balance sheet in the PIA Ratios. There are three key sections in the asset section and three in the liability and net worth section.

We've used a condensed format here, and this principle should hold true with most "condensed" forms of reporting. The major asset portions are:

Current assets

Fixed assets

Other assets

With these three sections we can summarize all that the firm has and holds as property.

Our liability section has two major sections: current and long-term. Long-term usually means the various forms of formal indebtedness that extend beyond the one-year limit. Current means those debts payable within the next 12-month period. There may be exceptions to this once in a while but we can't think of any we've seen this past 25 years or more. It really would be an "exception."

The equity section or ownership part or net worth section is a nightmare for the public accounting profession when it comes to consistent terminology. Give an honest job out for bid and you'll get as many different bids as there are estimators involved. So it is with "styles" of reporting net worth. What do you want the report to reveal? Do you have some particular message for the stockholder? Then inform your accountant and he'll design an honest way to tell it. Entire sections of accounting handbooks and many chapters in all levels of college accounting texts deal with the problem. We'll not be able to define it, much less solve it, in one chapter or a whole book.

Let's take this opportunity to look at the industry we represent while these two balance sheets are here before us. These profiles or averages for similar size firms—one a profit leader and the other one also in the race—show a few pertinent points worth our consideration. (See Exhibit 2.)

We could spend much time and space on the subject of ratios as they are used in the evaluation of the strengths and weaknesses of the firm. The PIA Ratios have an excellent section concerning this type of analysis. What we say would be at best a rerun of what Harris Margolis has highlighted in that report. This section of financial analysis had not received very much attention until the 1973 ratio study.

To those owners and operators who have to be all things to all people inside and outside their companies, it would be well worth their while to get a set of these studies to guide them through the complexities of accounting and financial management as it relates to our industry.

We shall use the same basic data by company size when reviewing the problems of evaluating the operating statement. Then you can match up the balance sheets of the medium-size profit leaders with their profit-and-loss statement. As there is a great difference in the equity section of the balance sheet—with a differential of over $139,000 or almost 80 percent more than the base equity of the "OTHER" firms—so there is a great difference in the Operating Profit of these two groups. Sales are nearly identical, yet the profit leader walks off with $105,300 net profit before taxes while the others just average $22,200 net. The 375-percent differential will be the subject of another chapter. Why is it? And where?

We have included Exhibit 3 for the primary purpose of establishing the validity of certain data that we will present from time to time. (There are far more than *just a few* who look at the PIA Ratio Studies as being not *too honest*.) These are based on remarks we've heard off and on for better than six years.

In order to prove a point once and for all, we sought out a completely impartial third-party report, made quarterly by the Federal Trade Commission for all classes of United States Industry. It is remarkable when you consider that PIA studies only some 1000 or so annual reports for the Ratio Study and the FTC selects a much greater number of firms for its total industry report. We have not made any attempt to reconcile these two reports, we really couldn't because we deliberately selected different dates, as well as the different data bases.

Our comparisons show some remarkable similarities, however. Total current assets for each group are very, very close, and the various sectional classifications within the total are generally quite close. We've noted an obvious classification difference within the fixed asset section, as our governmental accountants don't always agree with basic industry classifications. When combined with other assets, the fixed and other asset totals are very near each other.

Exhibit 1

Condensed Comparative Balance Sheet
For Profit Leader and Other Medium Size Printing Firms
At December 31, 1972

Assets	The Profit Leaders	The Other Firms
Current Assets		
Cash	$ 56,700	$ 24,700
Receivables	146,200	109,100
Inventories	61,800	45,500
Other Current Assets	23,400	19,200
Total Current Assets	288,100	198,500
Fixed Assets		
Machinery, Equipment and Real Estate	389,100	338,200
Less Accumulated Depreciation	199,500	184,700
Net Fixed Assets	189,600	153,500
Other Assets	29,000	16,400
Total Assets	$506,700	$368,400

Liabilities and Net Worth

	The Profit Leaders	The Other Firms
Current Liabilities		
Notes Payable	$ 24,600	$ 30,400
Accounts Payable	58,400	49,600
Other Current Liabilities	53,400	28,700
Total Current Liabilities	136,400	108,700
Long Term Liabilities	56,200	84,800
Total Liabilities	192,600	193,500
Shareholders' or Proprietors' Equity	314,100	174,900
Total Liabilities and Net Worth	$506,700	$368,400

Source: Absolute Data Section 1973 Printing Industries of America Ratio Study, for 45 Profit Leader Firms and 250 other Medium Size Printers.

Exhibit 2

Basic Variances Between
Medium Size Profit Leader Firms and Others, 1972

The Profit Leaders usually have:				Percentage of Others
More Cash	by	$ 32,000	or	129.6%
More Receivables	by	37,100	or	34.0%
More Inventory, Other Current Assets, and Other Assets	by	33,100	or	40.8%
More Net Fixed Assets	by	36,100	or	23.5%
More Total Assets	by	$138,300	or	37.5%
With Less Total Liabilities	by	900	or	.5%
Leaving the Profit Leaders with Far More Equity	by	$139,200	or	79.6%

Note: Sales were almost equal, P/L at $1000 less than Others, and both being almost equal in combined depreciation charges plus equipment rental costs: $400 variance, negligible or near perfect. These last two items will be included in the analysis of the same firms' 'average' profit and loss statements. (See the January 1974 issue of *Printing Impressions*.)

However, when we move down to the liabilities sections of the balance sheets we note some differences that can be either "reconciled" or explained by simple logic. Suppose that these two data bases were identical. Then it would logically seem to me, that notes payable had increased for the reason that the long-term notes (in total) at year-end 12/31/72 were now moved up within the one-year period of becoming due. Therefore they were reclassified. Long-term debt comprises the other half of these changes through a corresponding reduction.

Minor changes within detailed classifications account for variations within the major group. But look at the totals! Total Liabilities at 44.60 percent *for both groups!* Equity (regardless of internal detailed differences) stands at 55.40 percent—in total for both data bases!

Now as to the great differences between the data bases: the PIA Balance Sheet represents a little over $1 billion in assets for their total, or only 5 percent of the industry as represented by the FTC data covering over $21.2 billions in assets. As one who has spent the better part of his lifetime buried among the statistical mountains of dollars and percentages, it gives me a real comforting feeling to see such solid proof of validity for PIA. Some skeptics (or most for that matter) will still knock the ratios and other management tools. They will probably also cry about the fact that they aren't making the money old Dad did. And then, wonder why!

Exhibit 3

Printing and Publishing
Condensed Comparative Balance Sheets
as of 12/31/72 for PIA and 6/30/73 for FTC
(By Percentage of Total Assets)

	All Firms in 1973 PIA Ratio Study 12/31/72	Firms Selected by FTC Qtrly. Report 6/30/73
Cash	4.34%	9.00% (a)
Receivables—Net	28.50	22.50
Inventories	13.72	12.40
Other Current Assets	5.15	5.70
Total Current Assets	51.71	49.60
Fixed Assets: Net	42.04	31.60 (b)
Other Assets	6.25	18.80 (b)
Total Assets	100.00%	100.00%
Liabilities and Net Worth		
Notes Payable	5.54%	8.10%
Accounts Payable	11.59	13.70
Other Current Liabilities	9.04	6.40
Total Current Liabilities	26.17	28.20
Long Term Debt	18.43	16.40
Total Liabilities	44.60	44.60
Ownership: Equity	55.40%	55.40%
Total Liabilities and Net Worth	100.00%	100.00%

(a) Federal reports include Government Securities with cash.
(b) Obvious classification differences within these two basic sections. Combined PIA reflects 48.29% while the Federal Trade Commission shows 50.40% six months later.
Source: PIA Ratio Study for 1972/73 and Quarterly Financial Report for Manufacturing Corporations, Second Quarter 1973, Federal Trade Commission.

Chapter 6
Money Management Makes
More "Profit Leaders"

"As you stand and are counted,
you will first run into the group
who equate newness with wrongness.
If it's a new idea,
it's uncomfortable and they won't like it."
—Thomas J. Watson, Jr.
I.B.M. Chairman

Omar Khayyam expounded on much more than "a loaf of bread, a jug of wine and thou"—he also advised "Ah, take the cash and let the credit go, nor heed the rumble of a distant drum . . ."

Wouldn't it be nice if we could all do just that?

Last week we received the weekly mailing from a trade association. Worthy of note was the reminder to watch credit and collections. Times have brought us again to a period that will be marked by the move toward slower and slower payments. Even in good times, this becomes a management worry spot. "Charge it" has become a way of life. This way needs constant control or it gets out of hand, with the long-term result being that credit management deteriorates.

The 1973 PIA (Printing Industries of America) Ratio Study included the following warning: "*Collection period:* This is a disturbing area. The collection period for 'all firms' of 60.6 days is much too high an average. And these figures are up from last year's 57.6." That makes the change in collection time a full 5.2 percent on the downbeat side, in just one year! Not as bad as inflation . . . or is it?

For its profit leader firms, PIA reported in 1968 that the average period of collection took an even 51 days. In 1973 this period had moved up to a new total of 61.7 days—a 21-percent increase in five years, approximately 4 percent per year.

Before we try to figure out why, let's take a harder look at 1973 and what it cost the industry in time and effort as well as actual "lost" dollars. Let's consider a few key principles we must stay with if we are to avoid the narrow viewpoint of a statistical "counting house" philosophy.

What is the counting house philosophy of the balance sheet? For one thing, it considers the balance sheet as the house we live in. Most financial men go this route. The PIA Ratio Study is no exception. But everybody doesn't think that way. C. B. Randall, once president of Inland Steel, coined the term in his book *Folklore of Management* (1959). That's a book to be prized and re-read every few years to get us back on the track of reality. One myth has to do with preoccupation with a perfect set of figures within the balance sheet. Randall does not take the balance sheet for what most CPA's do. "Actually, a good balance sheet is like the foundation for a house," he says. "It is important, but nobody lives in it. Everything that counts happens above that level."

So, instead of comtemplating the navel of the balance sheet, let's look at some taken from our field that are not so perfect. Exhibit 1, while comparing averages with a full five-year timespan, does not reflect very consistent management decisions. These figures are taken from a total of 278 balance sheets and constitute a very stable base for statistical measurement, one quite acceptable by almost any standard.

Our pricing has been improved, as the average of sales has dropped by a full 10-percent margin while net profits are almost equal. So, the Profit-and-Loss Statements (not being considered here) would—or should— show a good measure of improvement. But we are concerned with cash and receivables in this effort. The average firm has decreased its cash position by better than 40 percent while increasing the receivables base by better than 30 percent. A goodly part of this is the result of carrying the customer a longer period of time. They are on the books 12 percent longer now than they were five years ago.

The write-off of bad debts, while being fairly high percentagewise, is not so great dollarwise, and thus it is better passed by without comment. The same may not be true of other size groups, as we shall see.

Move along now to Exhibit 2 so we can take an overview of the conditions among the giants of the industry. Here is where a good, critical analysis of long-term trends and policies can really pay off to the management man with the guts to break loose from the bonds of habit and apathy.

To be sure the base of this study is quite small in total numbers of firms, as it reflects only some 74 balance sheets. But the sum total of assets involved is a whopping $700 million. Again, it's a five-year timespan we are considering. What change has come to this largest size-grouping in the industry!

Exhibit 1

The 1973 Record for Firms with
Sales Between $25,000 and $500,000,
with Comparative 1968 Data

Average per Firm by Profit Leaders, Others, and *Total* Group

Classification	Number of Firms	Total Assets	Sales	Cash	Receivables	Bad Debts	Collection Period Days	Net Profit
1973 profit leaders	37	$181,000	$356,760	$22,440	$58,820	$1,750	60.3	$39,210
Other	110	200,000	368,180	12,390	58,030	1,215	57.5	10,730
Total 1973 Group	147	195,200	365,300	15,320	58,230	1,350	58.1	17,900
Total 1968 Group*	131	$212,010	$402,440	$21,000	$44,100	$61	51.8	$17,960
Percent 1973 over 1968**		(8.6%)	(10.2%)	(41.3%)	32.0%	(19.3%)	12.1%	(.3%)

Based upon Absolute Data Section of PIA Ratio Studies for years indicated.
Figures rounded off to nearest ten dollars.

*1968 Data not applicable for segregation of Profit Leader firms. However, a profit leader firm with that volume of sales would have generated $47,000 of profit vs. the total average of $17,960. The other relationships would hold true in the same general manner.

**(decrease)

Sales within this classification have, on the average, increased a full 106 percent over those of five years ago, *but net profits have only increased some 85 percent.* That shows how good pure volume is! (A few comments on that later.)

Our total assets, while increasing over 100 percent, have had a mercurial growth pattern. Our cash has dropped some 30 percent while our receivables have jumped almost 120 percent! Our bad debts have spiraled upwards at a better than 600 percent of what we were doing just five years ago! And our days of collection are up slightly beyond the 10-percent level.

What does it all mean to the large firm? If we stay with the 1973 figures we can see the value of certain decisions made at the management level: *The profit leaders have 30 percent more cash on hand with 39 percent fewer dollars tied up in accounts receivable.*

Some might be quick to point out that the profit leaders aren't so hot because they have had far more bad debts than the others. Well, that just might not be so. Let's consider this as an alternative explanation: What if the profit leader firms have recognized bad debts for what they are, and have written them off while the others are still packing them into accounts receivable and fooling nobody but themselves? If the accounts of the others were treated as realistically they, too, might be adding dollars to their bad debts as fast as sailors spend them on a shore leave.

In place of $69,300 for bad debts, perhaps, this figure should be $159,100 (at the same write-off as the profit leaders) and here's where the IRS enters the picture in cash flow. The difference between these two figures is some $89,300 in expenses against taxes. This means that at

Exhibit 2

The 1973 Record for Firms with Sales More Than $10,000,000, with Comparative 1968 Data

Average per Firm by Profit Leader, Others, and Total Group

Classification	Number of Firms	Total Assets	Sales	Cash	Receivables	Bad Debts	Collection Period (Days)	Net Profit
1973 profit leaders	12	$10,183,000	$16,625,000	$357,400	$3,225,100	$104,700	70.8	$1,734,000
Others	19	16,732,000	25,253,000	274,700	4,474,200	69,800	64.7	774,000
Total 1973 group	31	14,197,000	21,913,000	306,700	3,990,700	83,300	66.5	1,146,000
Total 1968 group*	43	$ 6,969,000	$10,619,000	$400,700	$1,818,900	$ 11,700	59.5	$ 617,000
Percent 1973 over 1968**		103.7%	106.4%	(30.6%)	119.4%	611.9%	11.2%	85.7%

Based upon Absolute Data Section of PIA Ratio Studies for years indicated. Figures rounded off to thousands and hundreds

*1968 Data not applicable for segregation of profit leader firms. However, on this sales volume the profit leader firm would have generated $1,012,000 net profit. Other relationships would also hold true in the same manner.

**(decrease)

least $44,000 could have been retained by the average large-size firm that is not a profit leader. Perhaps this is just one example of the top level management decision process that adds many dollars to cash flow over a long period of time. It has nothing to do with labor, production, pricing or other general management decisions. It is right at the door of the average treasurer or controller.

By a series of management decisions, what amount of dollars can be generated in cash flow as opposed to earnings from sales volume?

Would you believe it would be equal to the profits generated by another $1.7 million of sales, without all the attendant problems of personnel, production and procurement? How many sales people would you have to hire, train and motivate to get an additional $1.7 million in sales?

Remember this: *Volume sometimes does just the opposite of what it is supposed to do.* We have long preached the gospel of quality *vs.* quantity. It still holds true in many, many ways. The large profit leaders are running about $9 million less per firm in average number of sales dollars, yet they beat the others by almost a full million in profit dollars. This should speak loud and clear to boards of directors that something needs attention quickly!

If you think this loony and far afield, take a good, hard look at the small firms. The profit leader volume is a full $20,000 less in sales yet the profits generated are 265 percent greater! The reason is more than sales volume or production—it boils down to a long series of corrective management decisions. Added up, nothing approaches that tactic as being equal in leverage for three items: higher profits, more cash and more retained earnings.

A motivated management that controls change gets all three.

We haven't taken into account yet anything about the cost of money. How much does it cost us to finance such an additional burden of receivable dollars? Suppose that by hard work and diligent effort we could reduce the collection days by a full third—from 66.5 days down to, say 44.3 days? Would that save us money?

To begin with, we'd be able to cut $1,332,000 off our receivables. This, at 6 percent, would earn us in the financial income section at least $80,000. If we borrow money, the prime rate will be about 8 percent, or it'll cost us $106,000. Any way you view it, there are dollars of profit going by the boards in the credit area for the very large firms.

Don't say it can't be done. The large profit leaders among the smaller firms *are* doing it. This $80,000, at the large profit leader level, equals a cool $1 million in more sales effort. Once again: more people, more time, more effort, more paper-shuffling—for what? A better series of management policies on credit and collections may just be the beginning of adding that unseen force that produces more profits with less effort and far less over-all cost than most of the pack.

Is the rumble of the distant drum that most management listens to—more, more, more of sales, time and effort—the answer, or is that the drum we should NOT heed? Any time, we'll take the one that beats for cash flow and retained earnings.

Chapter 7
Zeroing in on Depreciation

"All things uncomely and broken,
all things worn out and old."
—William Butler Yeats

Code section 167 of the Internal Revenue Code covers depreciation. Commerce Clearing House Inc., which has prepared many of the books resting upon my office shelves, says this as an introduction to P 2900: "The law allows a deduction from gross income of a reasonable allowance for the exhaustion, wear and tear (including a reasonable allowance for obsolescence) of property used in a trade or business, or of property held for the production of income (but not inventory)."

Further on in this section the Supreme Court is quoted on this particular theory of accounting: "The theory underlying this allowance for depreciation is that by using up the plant a gradual sale is made of it. The depreciation charged is the measure of the cost of the part which has been sold. When the plant is disposed of after years of use, the thing then sold is not the whole thing originally used."

There are, of course, some basic rules for depreciation. We haven't time or space to review the many pages of the IRS code, but we should cover three items:

Item 1: Determination of property to be a capital item and therefore depreciable in the time-span of one year. If it is useful for production beyond 12 months you must capitalize it and not expense it in the period acquired.

Item 2: The first factor of the depreciation allowance is, *What did it cost?*

Item 3: What method shall we use to recover this cost (less salvage value)? Again we are in a time frame. How long and how much per accounting period?

When we look at the profit leader firm with $2,600,000 sales we find that he had total depreciation of 2.7 percent of sales. This amounts, for him, to about $70,700. But when we remove all direct material cost this item of depreciation becomes 4.9 percent of the total cost. The dollars haven't changed, just the base upon which we measure them.

Now what is the purpose of pouring these extra dollars of cost into future accounting periods? First off, we should recognize that these are not "extra" dollars of cost but cost dollars spread over the useful life of the item being considered.

It is best at the beginning to recognize this theory method of cost allocation for what it is—a method of cost allocation and not of valuation.

Depreciation has some very far reaching business decisions that rest upon it. Under our system of business we use this method to:

1. Help determine our year-end profit;

2. Play a leading role in figuring how much income tax we have to pay at year end;

3. Aid in setting norms for restrictive "valuation purposes" (exactly opposite what the code states!) for sale, purchase, consolidations, mergers, insurance purposes, and even local personal property tax use;

4. Evaluate worth for investment security purposes;

5. Guide alternative economic decisions (buy or lease, or get it done by a trade shop), and

6. Assist in most determination for the express purpose of *pricing our product* or service.

This of course leads us into the business of cost center application of depreciation as a controling element of cost.

In Exhibit 1 we have shown a 25x38" two-color perfector with costs for both one-and two-shift operation. We have shown the depreciation cost at the 10-percent level on the first shift and at 12.5 percent for two-shift operation. Total dollars assigned to depreciation (for costing purposes only) increase when we go to two shifts, but when divided between the two shifts they decrease on a per shift basis.

Most budgeted hourly cost studies released by regional or national trade associations use this method. I do also. So while I don't knock it, we have to recognize it for what it is: at best, a theory. It is a very practical supposition with a degree of flexibility to it.

We have experienced opposition to this method. Some want to include in their costs only the actual depreciation contained within their financial statement. If this be the case, the depreciation shown for two shifts will be identical in dollars to the one-shift cost, or the three-shift cost, for that matter.

I have seen profit leader firms take a pretty strong stand for this position. They maintain it gives them not only more accurate costing but also supplies a small leverage in pricing. And who is going to tell an 8-percent or 12-percent profit leader printer he is crazy?

Exhibit 1
Press Depreciation Costs
Miller TP 38, Two-Color Perfector, 25x38"
Capitalized at $115,000 with an hourly rate of $14.52

	One Shift	Two Shifts
Direct Labor	$23,275.56	$ 47,924.38
Fringes and Payroll Taxes	6,369.58	13,116.90
Indirect Labor and Supervision		
w/Fringes and Payroll Taxes	7,601.01	15,650.98
Total Factory Labor	37,246.15	76,692.26
Depreciation	11,550.00	14,437.50
Other Fixed Factory Cost	10,279.50	12,849.38
Variable Factory Costs	8,193.79	14,421.91
Total Factory Costs	67,269.44	118,401.05
G & A and Sales Costs	18,909.44	23,636.80
Total Costs	$86,178.88	$142,037.85
Hourly Costs @ 80% Productivity		
Factory Cost Only	$52.47	$46.18
Total Costs	67.22	55.40

We have long noted a close relationship between the classification of other fixed costs and depreciation. In most firms this holds true. However, when we come up against the argument of similar depreciation costs for both one- and two-shift operation, the theory bends in part and breaks down in another place. There is usually a slight rise in other fixed costs when we go to a two- or three-shift operation. Nothing like the rise in variable factory costs where supplies are concerned, but a slight rise nevertheless.

Exhibit 2 shows a broad scope of some ten cost centers; three in typesetting, two in platemaking, three in the pressroom and two in the bindery. These are random selections, all based upon 1974 rates in the east coast, metropolitan New York area. The ranges of cost relationships are very, very great. Some very interesting conclusions can be gotten from this exhibit.

What this may also point out is the fallacy of so-called budgeted hourly cost studies as they relate to the actual conditions among printing firms.

Any cost data study is, at best, a guideline toward your own effort. They cannot be accepted as gospel because they are *theory*, both in part and in whole.

Take, for example, the bottom two lines of Exhibit 2. The total depreciation for the ten randomly selected cost centers comes to 11.3 percent of their total cost. If this were true and perfect it would be closer to the 5-percent figure for the Total Corporation.

This difference is a part of the theory we are trying to explain. And this is true in every budgeted hourly cost study I have ever seen, my own included. Why the great difference, better than 125 percent, in depreciation?

For one thing, every budgeted hourly cost study we've ever seen has been tied directly to the then-current rate of inflationary dollars. All the equipment is generally priced at the current year level. The equipment represented in the corporate total is—as a group—usually five years old or older! Not so in the individual cost centers.

Now this points out something within your financial statements. Sales and materials and labor dollars are all at current rates and current costs. Depreciation dollars are a real "Duke's Mixture" of a little of everything. If one piece of equipment is in the tenth year of straight-line depreciation you have dollars in there from the base year of 1964. If a two-color 38" press then cost $45,000, we would be showing some $4500 annual depreciation cost. This could be compared to the $11,500 item in our Exhibit 2 for the two-color press. Within this one range we have a differential of over 150 percent from the true base!

Other costs will also be affected, such as values for personal property taxes, premiums for insurance, etc. We have here differentials that will greatly affect our pricing formula.

Now perhaps we can see the trueness of the old statement "Costs are facts but prices are policy."

We should also begin to get a handle on the fact that pricing is no easy thing. Yet in management circles I don't know of a more important series of decisions than those that affect the pricing of the product. Everything else can be A-1, the best. And if pricing is wrong, the whole thing goes down the drain.

Exhibit 2
Ten Random Selected Cost Centers
Profit Leader Firm Profile
Ten-Year Life Cost Center Equipment

Cost Center	One Shift Total Cost	Dir. Labor Str. Time	Depreciation	Other Fixed Cost
Proof Reader[1]	$ 30,208	$ 13,138	$ 120	$ 107
% of Total Cost		43.5%	.4%	.4%
Harris 1100[2] VDT	37,873	13,138	2,900	2,581
% of T/C		34.7%	7.7%	6.8%
Mergenthaler[2] VIP 7245-3A	49,728	13,138	7,200	4,728
% of T/C		26.5%	14.5%	9.5%
Stripper	28,433	12,038	120	107
% of T/C		42.3%	.4%	.4%
Kodalith Film Processor	32,884	12,038	1,735	1,543
% of T/C		36.6%	5.2%	4.7%
ATF Chief 17	28,549	11,510	610	543
% of T/C		40.3%	2.1%	1.9%
Miller TP 38[3] Perf. 2-color	86,178	23,275	11,500	10,279
% of T/C		27.0%	13.3%	11.9%
Harris 438	161,844	36,260	28,000	24,920
% of T/C		22.4%	17.3%	15.4%
Polar 90 Elect. 35" Cutter	25,587	9,313	1,395	1,241
% of T/C		36.4%	5.4%	4.9%
Macey Booklet[4]				
Master 12x18 17 Pocket	33,321	9,313	4,200	3,738
% of T/C		27.9%	12.6%	11.2%
Totals for Ten Basic				
Cost Centers	$ 510,605	$153,161	$57,780	$49,787
% of T/C		30.0%	11.3%	9.8%
Total Corp. Per P & L	$1,442,800	$570,200	$70,700	$62,900
% of T/C		39.5%	4.9%	4.4%

1. Proof reader and stripper min. cap. equip. @ $1200 inclusive
2. Leased equipment, five-year cost allocations
3. See Exhibit 1 for details of cost center
4. Costed with only one-man crew, loaders would need to be added as well as box-boys, etc.

After long and hard looks at this over-all problem of depreciation dollars and rates (and don't confuse the two) we have just about been persuaded that the best basis of costing and related pricing is to *use the actual costs* as reflected in your Profit-and-Loss Statement and Federal tax returns. They are the most honest, they are the most accurate. They can stand the critical eye and questions that become indefensible in other theories.

They do, however, present a problem, one of "recovery of cost" for equipment replacement. One purpose of this whole business of depreciation, from a practical view, is to enable the businessman to have funds set aside or allocated for the replacement of the equipment when it is past the stage of usefulness.

We'll cover this aspect of the function of depreciation later, picking up where we leave off.

Things that affect depreciation that we haven't yet touched upon are such items as: inadequacy, obsolescence, unusual damage, the estimating of service life of the asset, statistical methods of determination of useful life like actuarial, or turnover, or survivor curves, or graduated life tables, or the retirement frequency curve method, or probable life curves, the point rating method and revisions for correcting an incorrect method, and so forth.

Having done one or more of the above and having determined the first time-frame for asset life, how do we determine the cost?

Will it be property cost plus maintenance?

Or should it be cost less salvage?

Or maybe we need to reevaluate and go with the present value! If so we'll need an appraisal.

All this has to do with final rate determination. And then when it is all done we have to see if it will stand up to the IRS test.

Depreciation is far more complex than many owners and managers will admit.

The important thing to remember is that this one critical part of the total allocation process you have to know and control if you are going to properly cost your product. Better than 20 percent of your total cost (after materials) is in the region of depreciation and other fixed costs. That's too big a portion of the total cost dollar to give a quick brush-off. Perhaps this is one reason why so many printers don't know what their true costs really are.

The very wide variation in Exhibit 2 shows just what you are up against. Out of total cost, labor varies from a high of 43.5 percent total cost to a low of 22.4 percent. Depreciation has a bigger spread, going from a high of 17.3 percent to a low of 0.4 percent. Other fixed costs follows the footsteps of depreciation from a high of 15.4 percent to the low of 0.4 percent.

Please note the variation in labor from high to low at only about 95-percent variance with the lower base. In the other two cost areas the variation can be staggering. In depreciation it is over 4200 percent and in other fixed costs it is 3700-percent variation based on the lowest ratio!

On new equipment these last two items account for about 20 to 21 percent of total costs. On older equipment, beyond the five-year mark, this figure would easily drop to about 4-6 percent or lower! In any event, with such great cost differentials, it must be clear that the correct methods of costing are essential to pricing the product for a reasonable profit.

And the sad part of this whole discussion is that it has absolutely nothing to do with ink, or paper, or plates or presses, or quality, or webs or sheet feds . . . it's a matter of basic economics and finance.

H.L. Mencken said it years ago: "Nine times out of ten, in the arts as in life, there is actually no truth to be discovered; there is only error to be exposed."

Can this be applied to the graphic arts?

Chapter 8
Prime Navigational Aid
to Management:
Chart of Accounts

"Does he not keep account?
Indeed he does, most carefully.
Does he not enter small matters
in his books?
Indeed he does—everything."
—Marcus Tullius Cicero
81 B.C.

The report of a national public accounting firm to a large midwest manufacturer recently carried the following paraphrased item: "We call your attention to the importance of an adequate cost-accounting system as an indispensable prerequisite for the introduction of new and modern management techniques." The report went on to show that the firm had doubts about the client's system of overall accounting meeting these requirements.

Now consider this: the manufacturer is some fifty years in business, usually shows a fair profit, it has had a controller and chief accountant for some twenty years or more. The present controls in accounting were installed some thirty years ago. It was about the time that this manufacturer installed a punch-card accounting system. It was explained to the client firm that their cost system was very rudimentary. Costs for individual products and jobs were not available. Production data relative to various lines were gathered by some, but not by all, of the supervisory personnel. Selling prices were more often than not determined by some form of competitive basis. While operations overall seemed to be fairly profitable, present management saw no need for improvement.

What that CPA firm had done was fly the warning flag for their client. Let's hope that they took corrective action. Is this the kind of report you'd be earning were this firm to come in and audit your operations . . . not just prepare a "year-end statement"?

One big question . . . where would this corrective action most likely begin? And even more importantly, why there?

These two questions are often neglected by present management because of their not seeing the need to improve. Things are fair but could be better!

Good accounting is brought about by the planned, coordinated efforts of several management men. For it to be an adequate system there must be:

1. A properly organized system of account classifications, with each account being supported by suitable records.

2. There should be a complete system of methods and procedures to implement the total system.

3. This needs to be under the direction of a properly trained and experienced accounting executive who will see to it that items one and two are adequate and who shall be able, through a system of management reports, to interpret the results of operations both speedily and completely.

This effort will be directed towards the first of the three items above. This is a good beginning point for a better system. The chart of accounts of any firm is the framework within which all of the accounting and record keeping is constructed. Above all else we must see to it that all records are treated uniformly. That they are properly classified by type of business transaction, by function, by objective and even by area of accountability or responsibility. The final format of these uniform account classifications will take into consideration the size, the type of business, the need of management for certain information and the cost of getting that information. A one-man art shop does not have the needs of a five-hundred man web printer. Their individual charts of accounts will reflect these size differences.

In a one-man shop, either the owner or his outside accountant or bookkeeper will set up a very simple set of accounts. In larger firms it will almost always fall the lot of the controller/treasurer. Often outside aid comes from their accountants.

This chapter is not intended to replace basic texts in accounting. Complete and full definitions for each of these standard classifications can be found in any freshman level college textbook. The differences in variations among authors will be very slight. Some will be a bit more technical than others. We would suggest that if you have any difficulty in understanding these basic account classifications, that in itself should tell you that you are in need of professional help and should seek out the services of a local CPA.

Quite often in seminars I poke fun at the CPA's or what some in the profession call themselves . . . "number dummies". I tell people it means "Cleaning, Pressing and Alterations." And in a very subtle way it does, they *clean up the mess* of data and sloppy figures, they *press it all together* and *alter it* to fit the various forms required by local, state and federal agencies. But the smart money-makers I know use this professional breed for all they can. And it is well worth it. This is one way to make money by spending money.

The basic report known as the balance sheet is prepared from a partial listing of all these various accounts we have listed in our Exhibit 1. Part of them are used for the profit and loss account classifications.

Exhibit I
Simplified Chart of Accounts
for Small or Medium Printing firm.

Accounts	General Group of Accounts
Code Series	*Descriptions*
001 - 099	Unassigned - open
100 - 199	Assets of all types
200 - 299	Liabilities of all types
300 - 399	Ownership or Equity Accounts
400 - 499	Sales
500 - 599	Cost of Sales - Materials
600 - 699	Cost of Sales - Payrolls (Factory)
700 - 799	Cost of Sales - Factory Expenses
800 - 899	Cost of Sales - Administrative Exp.
900 - 999	Cost of Sales - Sales Expenses

All Balance Sheet accounts are to be found in the upper groups 100 through 399. All others are for the preparation of the profit & loss statement. Double entry bookkeeping and the financial statements are said to be "*in balance*". . when the Net Profit before Taxes from the P & L equals and balances out to the net change in the equity section of the balance sheet. It is this small profit or loss that makes the two become one. The differential is the total result of the P & L. In effect, the P & L could be run within the equity section of the balance sheet and the two could become one report.

Balance Sheet Account Classifications
Chart of Accounts
Assets

General series	sub class. code	Account Description
100	1 - 9	Petty Cash
		Undeposited Cash
		Cash in Banks
	10 - 19	Notes Receivable
		Accounts Receivable
		Allowance for Bad Debts
	20 - 29	Marketable Securities
	30 - 39	Inventories
		Raw Material
		(such as paper and direct press items)
		Work in Process
		Finished Goods
		Others
	40 - 49	Other Current Assets
		Prepaid Expenses
100	50 - 59	Real Estate
		Land
		Buildings
		Allowance for Depreciation
	60 - 69	Machinery & Equipment
		Direct and Indirect Production Equipment
		Allowance for Depreciation
	70 - 79	Other Fixed Assets
		Not listed above
	80 - 89	Other Non-current Assets

Balance Sheet Account Classifications
Chart of accounts
Liabilities

General Series	sub Class. code	Account Description
200	1 - 9	Notes Payable Within One Year
	10 - 19	Accounts Payable
	20 - 29	Taxes Payable
	30 - 39	Accruals
		Wages

	Interest
	Taxes
	others
40 - 49	Other Short Term Liabilities
50 - 59	Notes Payable Beyond One Year
60 - 69	Other Long Term Liabilities

Net Worth or Owner's Equity

300	Corporate Stock Accounts
	Corporation Surplus or Undivided Profits
	or
	Proprietary Capital Accounts

These are but a very simple guide to you and your CPA to get your accounting into line with what the industry as a whole has been using with more than limited success. The profit leaders who use this basic concept of accounts classification know what they are doing, know what has been done . . . and more important . . . know where they are going. This could be a part of the reason why.

A full and complete listing is available to each and every PIA member firm—it comes in the various mailings promoting the Ratio Study each year. It's bad enough to ignore the ratios and not participate but to ignore the good chart of accounts is even worse!

Chart of Accounts Operating Statement

General Series	Sub Class. Code	Account Description
400	1 - 49	Gross Billed Sales By Product Class or End Product
	50 - 99	Allowances & Returns By Product Class or End Product
500	1 - 9	Work In Process Inventory
	10 - 99	Materials Used in Production Paper Ink Carbon Glue
600	1 - 9	Factory Executives Salaries & Wages
	10 - 19	Direct Labor - Wages: Straight Time
	20 - 29	Direct Labor - Wages: Overtime
	30 - 39	General Factory Salaries & Wages

	40 - 49	Packaging, Shipping, and Delivery Wages
	50 - 59	Factory Payroll Taxes
	60 - 69	Factory Vacation & Holiday Pay
	70 - 99	Factory Fringe Benefits
700	1 - 49	Fixed Factory Expenses

Rent & Heat
Insurance on Real Estate & Property
Taxes on Real Estate & Property
Depreciation Buildings & Machinery & Equipment
Lease and Rental of Equipment

50 - 99   Variable Factory Expenses
Departmental Expenses and Supplies
Maintenance & Repairs
Other Indirect Supplies
Packing, Shipping & Delivery Expenses
General Factory Supplies & Expenses
Freight, Parcel Post
Utilities

800		Administration Expenses
	1 - 9	Executive Salaries, Bonuses etc.
	10 - 19	Office Salaries
	20 - 29	Payroll Taxes
	30 - 39	Fringes
	40 - 69	Other General Office Expenses
	70 - 79	Bad Debts / Financial Expenses
	80 - 89	Other Taxes, Income & Property
900		Selling Expenses
	1 - 9	Executive Salaries, Commissions, Bonuses
	10 - 19	Salesmen's Salaries, Commissions
	20 - 29	Office Clerical Salaries
	30 - 39	Payroll Taxes
	40 - 49	Fringes
	50 - 79	General Sales Expenses & Travel
	80 - 89	Advertising & Marketing Expenses

These basic accounts produce the two most important communication documents of the business life, the answers to the two questions: Where are we? This is answered by the balance sheet because it is a statement of condition as of a particular time. Question number two is "How did we get there?," answered by the profit & loss statement, which covers a broad scope of time and gives the information as to income, cost and profits.

Now where does this leave us as to the individual work stations? What do they contribute to the overall profitability of the firm? What do they cost us to operate for this period of time? None of the day-to-day operational, functional income/cost questions are answered by financial accounting. It just is not designed nor geared to perform that function. The only way out is to do cost finding and/or set up a series of internal accounts that will become a part of the financial record keeping. This latter is an *absolute out* for most firms under $5,000,000 in sales. Therefore we have to move to cost finding. This is what the general accounting profession calls what we in our industry term budgeted hourly costs. It is nothing new, other industries have had it for years under the term of machine hourly rates. So be it cost finding, or budgeted hourly costs or machine hourly rates, it is all in the family of cost accounting or near relatives to witchcraft and assorted prophetical philosophies. Well, not really *that* bad!

Balance Sheet (Medium Size Firm, 1974)
Assets (Chart of Accounts, Codes 100 - 199)

Current Assets:

Cash	$ 49,800
Receivables	139,800
Inventories	61,500
Other Current Assets	21,000
Total Current Assets	272,100

Fixed Assets

Machinery, Equipment & Real Estate	346,500
Less Accumulated Depreciation	187,600
Net Fixed assets	158,900
Other Assets	25,400
Total Assets	$456,400

Liabilities (Codes 200 - 299) and Equity (300 - 399)

Current Liabilities:

Notes Payable (Less than 1 year)	$ 15,000
Accounts Payable	58,800
Other Current Liabilities	46,800
Total Current Liabilities	120,600
Long Term Liabilities	66,500
Total Liabilities	187,100
Shareholder's or Proprietor's Equity	269,300
Total Liabilities and Owner's Equity	$456,400

Based upon 1974 Absolute Data Section PIA Ratio Study, medium size firm with $850,000 Net Sales and in the Profit Leader Group for this size class. All figures rounded off to nearest hundred.

In our *Exhibit 2*, we have shown the balance sheet of this average medium size profit leader with $850,000 in sales. This indicates a real healthy firm. We've shown the account classification codes for the chart of accounts to enable you to see where the various figures come from. We know this is *too basic* for the people who have had formal accounting in college classes, but the vast bulk of the printing industry is not so well blessed. Permit us this basic simplicity.

Exhibit 3.
Profit & Loss Statement

Chart of Accounts Number Series	General Accounting Account Description and Account Classifications with Sub-Totals and Totals	Amount to Nearest $100
	Sales Value of Production	$850,000
500's	Materials:	
	Paper	182,200
	Other Mat'ls & Outside Services	103,500
	Total Materials	285,700
	Value Added by Mfg.	564,300
600's	Factory Payroll	
	Direct Wages	191,700
	Supervision & Indirect Labor	39,300
	Factory Payroll	231,000
700's	Factory Expenses:	
	Fixed Costs	45,100
	Variable Costs	34,100
	Total Factory Expenses	79,200
	Factory Cost of Prod.	595,900
	Gross Profit	254,100
800's	Administration Exp.	82,400
900's	Selling Exp.	76,400
	Total Admin. & Selling Exp.	158,800
	Operating Income	95,300
	Other Income & (Expense)	5,000
	Net Income Before Federal Taxes	$100,300

Exhibit 3 is the standard format for most profit and loss statements, as used by those printers who use the standard PIA Chart of Accounts and follow the guidelines of the format of this statement as shown in the Ratio Studies. All too few printers use it. Some do, and to great advantage we might add. It is clear, concise and informative on both controllable and non-controllable data. And if you don't think some of these overhead items are non-controllable, you don't have a healthy respect for the laxity of much of management. Overhead grows like a cancer. If not observed in due time and held in check it is every bit as deadly to the corporate body.

Note the pattern of the computerized cost printout, how it follows the basic format of the profit & loss statement. This is the format we recommend as it is so much easier to understand and to reconcile by departments into the operating statements. In Exhibit 4 we've taken a VIP 4836 and worked it into the financial structure of a profit leader printing firm based upon sales mix of $2,600,000 and data covering a one-year period. These are not the overhead allocations that would accrue from the use of this 1974 mid-size $850,000 sales base printer. However, they wouldn't be off very much. This is shown as an *example* only. Don't take these totals and costs as applicable to mid-size 1976 printer. This is from the *Handbook of Operating Costs and Specifications for Phototypesetting Equipment* published by North American Publishing Co. in the spring of 1975.

In the next chapter we will discuss completed financial statements and the task of evaluating them. What do they show? Where do we need to put our corrective effort? How to take them as a beginning point for our cost finding?

Just how important this "cost finding" business is can be best shown in a look at value added. When the cost of materials is removed from our P & L, the balance of our costs reflect a portion of prime costs (the non-materials half) and the little bit of direct factory costs called depreciation. The big bulk of what's left is overhead!

In the Exhibit 3 we've used herein, the amount of pure overhead is $252,500 while direct labor and depreciation are only $216,500. The real import of this is that for every $1.00 of either depreciation or direct labor input into any production during this year . . . . these firms also had $1.17 of *overhead.*

When it came to pricing the product these profit leader management men did not ignore that factor. To have done so would have pushed them down to a lower profit level with the big bulk of printers of this size. The dual problem of either ignorance of the fact *and* cost of overhead or the lack of an accurate figure as to what overhead really is causes more profit loss than any other single factor. One produces improper pricing from ignorance (which means looking over or past a problem), the other improper pricing for *lack of cost data.*

Good companies cannot survive with either of these two monsters. And good, strong growth is much more than survival! Think about it.

Exhibit 4

TEXT PHOTOTYPESETTERS	Handbook of Operating Costs and Specifications for Phototypesetting Equipment		

MERGENTHALER LINOTYPE CO. VIP 4836 M*		ONE SHIFT	TWO SHIFTS
CAPITALIZED $13,700	DIRECT LABOR – STR. TIME	$ 13,138.20	$ 27,196.07
HRLY. RATE $ 8.10	FRINGES & PAYROLL TAXES	3,163.12	6,548.81
	IND. LABOR & SUPERVISION	4,179.66	8,652.19
	TOTAL FACTORY LABOR	20,480.98	42,397.07
	DEPRECIATION	2,740.00	3,425.00
	OTHER FIXED FACTORY COSTS	2,438.60	3,048.25
	VARIABLE FACTORY COSTS	3,558.98	6,778.31
	TOTAL FACTORY COST	29,218.56	55,648.63
	G&A AND SALES COSTS	8,213.34	10,266.68
	TOTAL COST	$ 37,431.90	$ 65,915.31
	BUDGETED HOURLY COSTS		
	FACTORY COST ONLY 80%	$ 22.51	$ 21.44
	70%	25.74	24.51
	60%	30.03	28.60
	TOTAL COST AT 80%	28.84	25.39
	70%	32.98	29.04
	60%	38.47	33.87

Chapter 9
Business Ratios:
Navigational Aids to the Profit Land

"Whatever is felicitously expressed
risks being worse expressed:
It is wretched taste to be gratified with mediocrity
when excellence lies before us."

—Isaac D'Israeli

In the summer of 1975 we ran a series of one-day seminars on the subject of cost control and profitable pricing. During the course of these round table workshop discussions more than once we heard evidence of the disbelief in the validity of the PIA Ratio studies. Now these words of critical comment didn't come from some blue collar craftsman member of a graphic arts union who might be inclined to pooh-pooh the idea of such low levels of profit. These comments came from controllers and treasurers of some pretty fair-size firms.

Though the PIA Ratios are well beyond the Golden Anniversary stage they are still not yet accepted either as 1) fact or 2) as the best of the management tools available today.

Just a few short years ago, in 1969, the ratios themselves entered into a new phase of use. But rather than us saying what we think let the ratios speak for themselves:

"The 1968-69 Ratio Study (that is now almost ancient history, isn't it?) is different from earlier editions. It represents the second stage of our Ratio Study redesign intended to make the study a tool as basic to printing management as a pica gauge is to a compositor. This year the Ratio Study is issued in a standard financial accounting format so that every printing company, regardless of its cost accounting system, can apply these figures and use them without difficulty." You have to know other industries and other fields of business to appreciate the impact of that single factor upon our trade!

And they are getting better all the time. This is the remarkable thing. Each year sees some improvement.

If we were able to go back some 50 years we would see these tools of management as they were first developed. In the 1925 ratio study you could read: "The Financial story of an industry is best told in its financial ratios, and cost analyses. Management can no longer rely solely on personal observation and impressions when formulating business plans and policies."

Now this personal observation fly-by-the-seat-of-the-pants bit is what I note that most low profit firms are still doing. Fifty years later! And if all goes well there will still be a few losers around doing it fifty years from now. Traditional habits are difficult to change.

Continuing with the age-old, white-bearded advice from 1925, the opening statement of the ratio of that year continues: "All classified expense items bear more or less definite relationships to each other so that ratios representing these relations become bases for the determination of policies and procedures." Now that sounds like something from a 1975 IBM or Xerox or Singer Computer Systems manual. Yet the principle is age-old. And still everyone doesn't buy it. But the winners do. And they profit from it handsomely.

Jump forward in time now, as they do on these TV science fiction dramas . . . let it be suddenly 1935 . . . FDR is President. Hitler is still pretty small potatoes in Europe and in the Ratio Study of that year we find this: "By the adoption of a Standard Classification of accounts, statements derived from accounting records of members with plants of all sizes are readily combined in groups according to size or nature of business or any other desired combination."

The term Standard Classification of Accounts is what marks an industry as "coming of age." It knows where it is and where it is going. Individual firms within that industry can and should have the same advantages of standardization. This means we can compare apples and apples, or grapes and grapes, or web presses with web presses, or trade typesetters with trade typesetters. We are not alone in the concrete jungle, but through cooperative effort aiding and assisting each other to a higher level of productivity and profit.

Still some people sit around and say it is all phoney. At the end of World War II the 1945 Ratios had this to say: "The Printing Industry has the honor of being the first industry to undertake seriously the establishment of uniform cost and accounting methods. The United Typothetae of America in 1910 developed a uniform and standard system for the Printing Industry from which has been derived an effective method of securing comparable basic information concerning the financial and operating aspects of the

Printing Industry. The financial statements furnished by the industry are a contribution to the unified solution of the industry's problems and by this cooperation the individual member gains from others the collective experience of the industry."

That should be endowed in each graduating member of every graphic arts course in every college and university. That principle is more important than much time on the craft details that future members of the management team must master. For in much of our training of future management personnel in our industry we are still geared to the guilds of the middle 16th century.

Even those words are some 30 years old . . . now fast getting older. Yet they are as true as when first stated. It seems strange indeed that Dun & Bradstreet in their Business Education Division text *Patterns for Success in Managing a Business* has as the last chapter: "Key Business Ratios" wherein they spell out such items as:

Collection Period Ratios
Current Asset Ratios
Cash or Accounts Receivable or Notes or all three!
Current Debt Ratios
Fixed Asset Ratios
Funded Debt Ratios
Inventory Ratios
Net Profit Ratios
Net Sales Ratios
Sales to Iventory Ratios
Net Working Capital Ratios
Tangible Net Worth Ratios
Turnover of Net Worth Ratios
Turnover of Net Working Capital Ratios
and on and on and on by variation
and by line of business . . .

Is this all new stuff? Not on your life. The edition I have is the third printing (1970). Perhaps they are printing number seven or eight by this time, if previous editions reflect the buying habits of the American businessman these past five years.

Ratios travel in higher math circles of proportion and simultaneous equations . . but don't be frightened—when explained in all their basic simplicity it comes out like this: The ratio of two numbers is the quotient of the first divided by the second. Period, end of explanation. And that, believe it or not, is all of third grade math! How very elemental, how very simple to understand.

Peter Drucker in his latest masterpiece: *Management - Tasks - Responsibilities - Practices* states in the chapter on control, "Controls and Management" the following specifications for controls: That in order for the manager to control he must have controls . . . and that they in turn must be of seven specifications. They must be 1) economical, 2) meaningful, 3) appropriate, 4) congruent, 5) timely, 6) simple, and lastly 7) operational.

As a series of controls for management control the ratios from and for our industry fit that bill of materials perfectly.

What really gets me is the realization that some trade association executives in various regionals of PIA either don't understand their basic simplicity or write them off as nil for their members, for all the locals and regionals don't actively support and participate in these studies as they should. Those that do can profit greatly from their participation. Those that don't perhaps are unaware of what they are missing. Less than one firm in six of the PIA membership participates. This in itself further upholds the old 80/20 law of profits and involvement. Those that need help the most fail to seek it. It has always been that way.

For many, many years the bible of the accounting profession has been *The Accountant's Handbook* by W.A. Paton, Professor of Accounting at the University of Michigan and called by many the number-one man of the number dummies among us. This first book of the bookkeepers and accountants, comptrollers, and controllers and assorted figure people has always featured the PIA ratios as a classic example for use in the chapters on statement analysis. Surely there must have been a reason for it. You'll find this particular book in the library of every senior partner of every one of the big eight accounting firms. That's the kind of book it is.

But we have men within our own trade, men who have sometimes been trained in their profession after college years by periods of time with these big eight firms, who still scoff and say, "Oh, they are unrealistic." What limited insight, what lack of understanding. What disregard for fine financial tools of their trade.

Rules of thumb are great for guesstimates, but for fine financial planning, look to your own firm's ratios and those of the industry you represent. You'll find no other finer gauge of production values, of operational cost structures and of guidelines into the higher plateaus of the promised profit land. The winners make it all the way. Some without the ratios, but most of them get there with the aid of those statistical road maps. Once you try it, you'll wonder how you ever made it blind!

Chapter 10
Profit Principles Between
the Lines of the P & L Statement

"A principle of policy, once established,
be it sound or unsound, is almost sure,
through evolution, to exert an influence
far beyond that created at the
time of its original inception."

—Alfred P. Sloan, Jr.
Chairman, General Motors Corp.

Old Professor H.A. Finney, Ph.D., CPA and one-time head of the accounting department of Northwestern University has probably done more in his time to teach the "Number Dummies" among us than any other person. His textbooks have become classics to the profession. In one of these old texts he has the following as an introduction to basic accounting theory: "Our economic system is organized around and is actuated by the profit motive. Profits are made by furnishing goods or services to customers and clients at prices in excess of the related costs."

We'll not dwell on accounting theory, just the problems of printers who don't observe the last part of the above quote. The profit-and-loss statement is one of the two most basic management reports. It comes second because it is included in summary format (sometimes just a one-line entry) on the balance sheet under the net worth section.

It might be a lot more fun and excitement to write some heavyweight stuff outlining the fundamental sins of management—and I do believe there are a few—but that we'll have to pass up for a more analytical study of what are the results of these sins of omission and commission.

Where do we make a buck under this economic system and, more important when it comes to cost, just where are we losing money? *How* it is lost is a return to the sins of management.

First of all we've used as a set of averages the figures from the 1973 Printing Industries of America (PIA) Ratios. That has been our base. We presented in Chapter 5 an analysis of balance sheets for profit leader medium-size firms with that of the rest of the group. We showed a consistency of asset value in excess of one over the other. The ones with the excess of assets at their call were within the profit leader group. They also had less liabilities, resulting in far more equity.

Now to the chicken-and-egg bit. Which comes first—does a string of good, consistent profit years build up assets, or does a strong asset position result in strong profits? On the whole, consistently strong profit years build up strong asset positions. Not the reverse. We've been on client assignments where a strong asset-oriented firm was depleted by improper management, as a few very poor P & L statements showed. Assets were milked away, for good!

Exhibit 1 shows a dollar comparison being made of two companies, one a profit leader and one a firm in the "also ran" group. There being 45 of the first and 250 of the second, the rule-of-thumb of 20/80 remains true in this case. The first 45 net out better than $4.7 million of final profits while the other 250 firms total out at about $5.5 million. How each individual firm makes out—on an average—is shown on the schedule of profit and losses (Exhibit 2).

First and foremost of the seven major areas that deserve management's attention is the area of basic production as found within the direct labor portion of the factory payroll. Over 50 percent of our differential (or variance) occurs within this one item. Number two will surprise many in that it occurs in the area of other materials and outside purchased services.

The third area is financial income, or expense. Number four is the fixed cost area of factory expense; numbers five and six are seemingly well out of place, as these two are usually whipping boys of any management cut-back. How does sales expense and general and administrative expenses strike you for these *low, way-down positions?* Last on the list is paper costs. Sort of dispels what we generally hear when a bunch of printers get together to swap lies, doesn't it?

Now let's examine this list in the details our supportive schedules show.

Before so doing, however, it might be wise to spend a little time with our Exhibit 2, for while this is an untitled item it may well be a very new, important management principle for some of our readers. This principle of management by exception needs to be followed by every level of management within the graphic arts—or any other business, for that matter.

The management-by-exception principle means you put your worry, time, effort, and the same *from all key employees,* upon those areas where improvement is absolutely necessary to the general welfare of your company.

Exhibit 1
Medium Size Firm Comparative Profit and Loss Statement
Year Ended December 31, 1972

	Average Profit Leader Firm		Average "Other" Medium Firm	
	Amount	Percent	Amount	Percent
Sales Value of Product	$917,800	100.00	$918,800	100.00
Materials used:				
Paper	181,900	19.82	185,900	20.23
Outside purchases and other	123,700	13.48	132,700	14.44
Total material	305,600	33.30	318,600	34.67
Factory payrolls	248,700	27.10	294,100	32.01
Fixed factory expenses	51,700	5.63	58,900	6.41
Variable factory expenses	43,800	4.78	43,700	4.76
Total factory expenses	95,500	10.41	102,600	11.17
Total factory cost	649,800	70.81	715,300	77.85
Gross Profit	268,000	29.19	203,500	22.15
General and administration expenses	86,300	9.40	90,800	9.88
Sales expenses	81,300	8.86	87,400	9.51
Total G & A and sales	167,600	18.26	178,200	19.39
Operating income	100,400	10.93	25,300	2.75
Financial income or expense	4,900	.54	(3,100)	(.34)
Net profit before taxes	$105,300	11.47	$ 22,200	2.41

Source: Absolute Data Section, PIA Ratio Study, 1973. Information based upon 45 leader firms and 250 others in medium size, range with sales of $500,000 to $1,500,000.

Exhibit 2

Where Are We Failing to Control Cost?	Management Problem Area Number	Variance or Dollar Differential	Percent of Total Differential
Factory Payroll	1	$45,400	54.6%
Outside purchases and other materials	2	9,000	10.8
Other income and expenses (financial)	3	8,000	9.6
Fixed factory expenses	4	7,200	8.6
Sales expenses	5	6,100	7.3
General and administrative expenses	6	4,500	5.4
Paper	7	4,000	4.8

Note: The total of variances equals more than 100 percent, this resulting from some of the offsetting variances in a plus condition. Each variance may be traced to Exhibit 1 for detail and Exhibits 3 and 4.

If we were to follow the above principle and correct only one item for a low profit firm it would be, of course, in the area of factory payroll. All too often we are prone to jump to the conclusion that this is due to the difference between the open and union shop. This is not always so. One firm that we are very well acquainted with stands in the high profit area and is constantly negotiating with five different unions. These union people are highly skilled, properly motivated and very competently managed. Note that all of the other variances put together will not equal number one.

If we examine the other schedules, the same principles will be seen to hold true. Exhibit 3 shows hardly any difference in the totals of variable factory expenses. Therefore, if the totals show no variance, why worry about the details?

You'd be far better off putting fixed expenses under the critical eye of some member of top management. What seems a major area of difference here in depreciation isn't exactly what it appears to be. The profit-leader firm, with a total of $30,700 for both depreciation and rental of equipment, is only $400 better in this category than the low-profit firms. But an interesting by-product might reveal itself here: rental charges for equipment (or leased equipment) are twice as high with the profit leaders as with the low-profit group.

Differences of a minor nature exist in both administrative and sales expense. As we stated previously, these two general categories receive the first of any budget cut-backs when belts have to be tightened.

We had originally thought that we would present here a one-page summary P & L with budget guidelines, year-to-date figures and variances. However, you will see these data in Chapter 11.

Several years ago we wrote an article jokingly called "The Hughes Hypothesis." It went something like this: "Most firms that are in the high-profit column are constantly trying to improve their profit position through every form of assistance available. Most low-profit firms are too busy with sales volume and related problems to spend the necesary time to get out of the survival rut and begin making a systematic approach to higher-profit land."

Among the PIA Ratio Study participants we know, there are at least 250 firms that obviously need help. The proof of the pudding is that these 250 companies have a 2.41-percent net profit before taxes. And this is why I believe our industry is a little sick. I could be wrong, but I don't think so.

Exhibit 3

Schedule of Factory Payroll Costs

	Profit Leader		Other Medium Firms	
Executive salaries	$ 12,000	1.30%	$ 14,200	1.55%
Direct labor wages	182,400	19.87	221,600	24.12
General factory wages	22,900	2.50	21,100	2.30
Packing and delivery	8,700	.95	9,100	.99
Payroll taxes	8,300	.90	12,000	1.33
Employee benefits	14,400	1.58	15,900	1.72
Total factory payrolls	$248,700	27.10%	$294,100	32.01%

Schedule of Factory Expenses

	Profit Leader		Other Medium Firms	
Fixed Cost				
Rent and heat	$14,000	1.53%	$17,800	1.94%
Insurance, real estate and property	3,200	.35	4,400	.48
Taxes: property	3,800	.41	5,600	.61
Depreciation	24,700	2.69	28,100	3.06
Rental equipment	6,100	.65	3,000	.32
Total Fixed Costs	$51,700	5.63%	$58,900	6.41%
Variable Costs				
Department supplies and expenses	$18,000	1.98%	$ 19,500	2.12%
Packing and delivery supplies	11,100	1.22	8,700	.95
General factory supplies	14,500	1.58	15,500	1.69
Total variable expenses	43,800	4.78	43,700	4.76
Total factory expenses	$95,500	10.41%	$102,600	11.17%

Exhibit 4

Schedule of General and Administrative Expenses

	Profit Leader		Other Medium Firms	
Executive salaries	$28,100	3.06%	$28,700	3.12%
Office salaries	25,000	2.72	26,000	2.83
Payroll taxes	2,100	.23	2,100	.23
Employee benefits	3,600	.39	4,200	.46
General office expenses	23,300	2.54	23,500	2.56
Allowance for bad debts	2,700	.29	4,600	.50
Other taxes	1,500	.17	1,700	.18
Total administrative cost	$86,300	9.40%	$90,800	9.88%

Schedule of Sales Expenses

	Profit Leader		Other Medium Firms	
Executive salaries	14,300	1.56	16,400	1.78
Salesmen salaries and commissions	39,100	4.26	40,900	4.45
Office clerical, salaries	5,300	.58	5,800	.63
Payroll taxes	1,300	.13	1,900	.21
Employee benefits	3,400	.37	2,900	.32
General and travel expenses	15,000	1.64	15,700	1.71
Advertising	2,900	.32	3,800	.41
Total selling expenses	$81,300	8.86%	$87,400	9.51%

Chapter 11
Confusing Semantics
of Cost

"If language is incorrect,
then what is said is not meant.
If what is said is not meant,
then what ought to be done remains undone."
—Confucius

The Queen in *Alice in Wonderland* was expounding upon the difficulties of her country: "A slow sort of country! Now, here, you see, it takes all the running you can do to keep in the same place. If you want to get somewhere else, you must run at least twice as fast as that!"

Was the old queen speaking about our industry in a year of shortages? She almost describes the present circumstances many find themselves in, what with the added problems of stiff competition, an ever-widening shortage of devoted and skilled craftsmen and salesmen. Our people problems, even in a period of higher unemployment, never seem to be completely solved.

Just as persistently, in every management meeting, comes the old bugaboo: "What shall we do to control our costs?" If it is not that exact question, then it is some close variation of it.

We've prepared two basic exhibits. One shows a format of a single page of financial reporting of use to management because it gives the key points as well as comparative data from the year-to-date budget and that of the previous year. The second exhibit shows a graphic picture of what we need to control—but first understand—in order to run twice as fast and get where we want to go. We'll never reach our goals without these cost elements under control. Never! I have yet to see a profit leader firm that ignored these various cost elements. They live with them and, above all, *control* them.

Taking our Exhibit 2 as a picture of the total sales value of production for a small printer as revealed in the 1973 PIA (Printing Industries of America) Ratio Study, we see a tiny part of our over-all problem. It is one of confusion and misunderstanding over terminology. We are the victims of a real language barrier. And in good part it is of our own making.

One can look rather objectively at the over-all picture of what happens with income and cost, and can usually break these two factors down into three parts: Income from sales, cost of those sales, and the resulting profits. Very simple and very basic.

But we've become sophisticated. Where three will not be enough, will six be twice as good? Or will nine different parts be three times better? When it comes to what is "enough," we are of the opinion that, for the highest level of management reports, you need more than the number shown in Exhibit 1. These are the essentials for the top-level decision makers.

Actually, we really have only six major cost elements and a set of combinations of these six, plus some differentials to equal all, as shown in our Exhibit 1.

We start off with sales value of production as it is made up of sales (shipped and billed) plus or minus the change in the value of finished inventory and work in process. These items really need not be shown on the over-all final reporting document to the highest levels of management. We show them here for the tie-in that some will make with the PIA Ratio forms. Then come the four main factory cost items:

Material Cost is broken down between paper and other costs. The other costs being further broken down by ink and direct press supplies and out-side purchased services. If a printer has a press operation only, then perhaps this one line in the summary report will be the total of various accounts for such items as type and art, platemaking and camera, and bindery and other finishing operations.

Factory Payrolls represent the largest single element in our cost structure. There are four parts to this element: Direct labor at the various cost centers and their related fringes and payroll taxes. The other parts are made up of indirect labor and supervision together with their related fringes and tax contributions by the company. Of course, within the books of account, in that portion of data called "payroll distribution," there may be charges that find there way into a multiplicity of accounts.

Fixed Factory Expenses are usually made up of depreciation and other types of "fixed cost." These are not fixed in the exact, literal sense of the word but are the kinds of costs that time and day-to-day production decisions do not affect. They just remain the same regardless of the amount of production or lack of it.

Variable Facotry Expense, however, follows the production cycle very closely, as it increases such supply and miscellaneous charges also increase.

Administration or office expenses and sales expenses complete the picture. And there we have the basic six cost elements. But from these six, or parts thereof, we can derive at least three times that number in names and terms that accountants and cost accountants use on a day-to-day basis, and these terms leave most members of the management cold! Very cold!

Exhibit 1

Monthly Report of Operations: June 1974 and Year to Date Comparative

	Monthly Budget	Current Month Amount	Ratio	This Year to Date Amount	Ratio	Last Year to Date Amount	Ratio
Sales (shipped and billed)		$212,000		$1,305,600		$1,185,400	
Net change in inventory		16,000		18,400		12,800	
Sales value of production	$220,000	$228,000	100.00%	$1,324,000	100.00%	$1,198,200	100.00%
Material cost	32.90%	72,980	32.01%	434,140	32.79%	385,940	32.21%
Factory payroll cost	30.90	70,540	30.94	410,700	31.02	380,430	31.75
Fixed factory expenses	5.15	11,810	5.18	70,170	5.30	62,310	5.20
Variable factory expenses	5.00	11,220	4.92	64,880	4.90	60,510	5.05
Total factory cost	73.95	166,550	73.05	979,890	74.01	889,190	74 21
Gross profit	26.05	61,450	26.95	344,110	25.99	309,010	25.79
General administrative	7.29	17,310	7.59	97,050	7.33	88,430	7.38
Sales expenses	7.18	16,870	7.40	92,940	7.02	86,390	7.21
Total cost of operation	88.42	200,730	88.04	1,169,880	88.36	1,064,010	88.80
Net profit from operations	11.58%	$ 27,270	11.96%	$ 154,120	11.64%	$ 134,190	11.20%
Orders entered this period		$208,600		$1,298,600		$1,186,800	
Backlog of orders		213,400		213,400		204,100	
Average productivity rate production per $1.00 factory payroll input	$ 2.1715	$ 2.1976		$ 2.1667		$ 2.1351	

Source: Various PIA (Printing Industries of America) Ratio Studies of 1971, '72 and '73. For example purposes only. All ratios given are unweighted averages of profit-leader firms for the last three years.

Let's examine some of these terms as they affect our industry.

A term we don't use very much is "prime cost," which equals the total of direct materials plus reproductive labor costs. In graphics for the most part this would include paper, ink, direct press supplies, outside services and direct labor in the production departments. As a general rule, when we speak of direct labor costs or any type of salary or wage costs we usually mean "fringes" included.

In another case, when a printer uses the term "overhead" just what does he mean? Is it factory overhead or total overhead? There is better than a 100-percent dollar differential there, and very worthy of pinpointing as to definition.

Factory cost, prime cost, and conversion cost are all different. And all three overlap each other to the utter confusion of the non-accounting member of the management team who gets into a bind when informed that he must begin to gather data for his department budget. Is it any wonder that the final reports of accountants are looked upon with more than a slight bit of suspicion?

Manufacturing expenses and manufacturing overhead, though similar terms, are not at all the same. One is but a part of the other. But to the shift superintendent or the plant manager it becomes another weary task of keeping up with a play on words.

Total overhead and manufacturing overhead are items presenting another example of sound-alikes representing vast differences in cost dollars. One is almost always twice as big as the other, which it encompasses. Oh yes, the men in accounting usually know these terms all by heart—but does your line management in the shop understand them? Whose tools are they?

When we get into the area of pricing it becomes even more clouded as some words change *without any dollar change*. What we call standby costs in economics can be *called fixed costs by many accountants*.

But when you get into the development of graphs and charts and the determinations of break-even points, what is fixed cost on the accounting statement is not the fixed cost of production-price relationships. Not at all.

The true fixed cost when determining break-even takes in a bit of direct labor, a goodly portion of supervision, all the "fixed" cost from the Profit and Loss statement and some of administration and some of sales expenses. These are what the economists call "standby costs."

Some day perhaps PIA will feature some portion of these cost elements as they did value added by manufacturing. This was the key point of the 1969 convention. However, the old expression "value added" sounds like some cold fish from the Department of Commerce and hasn't got much appeal and glamour about it. Therefore let's call it something else. They defined it properly at the convention: "Inside sales are the dollars of sales, or billings, minus the cost of paper and outside purchases."

The idea of contribution of profit by analysis was an important part of that particular effort. And after all, that is just what management reports are all about.

But in order to get that we have to recognize that in the words and terms we use there is a great deal of confusion.

Owen D. Young, who served as chairman of the board of General Electric for many years, said, "The commonest article of commerce is misinformation about fundamental things." This is our problem in the printing industry. I have seen many printers get uptight over the matter of "mark up" on paper and outside services, then pay very little regard to markup on their own *conversion costs.* Yet—be honest—which is more important?

When nine different elements can produce at least 22 different terms and meanings, then something needs some attention in regard to terminology standardization. Who's to do it? PIA? National Association of Printers and Lithographers? The National Association of Accountants? The various CPA's who serve the industry? Or will we face up to it, that *very little will be done* to make it easy for us and therefore we'll have to learn to change and adjust to conditions as will all our various management team members?

Let's come right down to the very bedrock of what management is all about: Isn't it to *manage change* and to *make the proper adjustments*?

It is a tribute to all members of management that in this critical area, *on the whole*, we survive because this is done. Those who can't be flexible and bend with the changes are like the trees whose limbs snap off in high winds. Only the ones that bend make it to full maturity. Think about it.

Exhibit 2
Cost Elements & Profit Leader Profile Small Printer — 1973

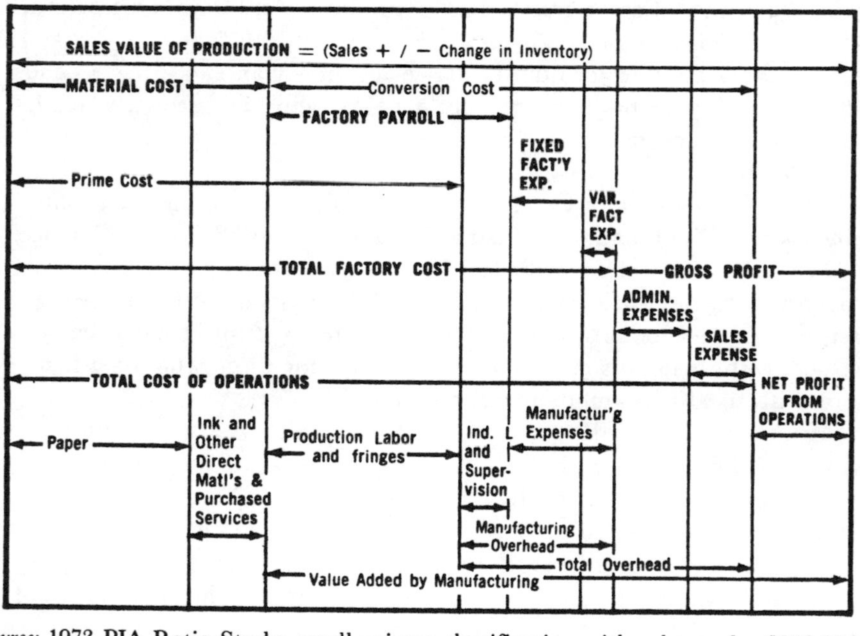

Source: 1973 PIA Ratio Study, small printer classification with sales under $250,000. Elements shown to scale. Capitalized items correspond to various lines in Exhibit 1.

Chapter 12
That Old What-Not Factor and Profit Control Plans

> "Amid a multitude of projects,
> no plan is devised."
> —Publilius Syrus
> 42 B.C.

The personnel director looked at the applicant and asked, "Where did you attend college?"

"At State Subnormal U., sir."

"Well, what did you study in the Printing Management course there?"

"Reeling and Writhing, of course, to begin with," the Mock Turtle replied, "and the different branches of Arithmetic: Ambition, Distraction, Uglification and Derision."

The personnel director quickly dialed a number and in a few seconds said, "Sam, tell your brother we've got a new Pricing Department Head, then come over and meet him."

Fade out.

Most printing executives on their way to the top have majored only in the Double D's of math—the Distraction and Derision School of Finance.

What do we mean with all this? Too many owners and managers of smaller and medium-size firms are distracted by costs of yesterday being fitted into sales of tomorrow. The other kinky major subject has been Derision, with its minors of contempt and scorn for those who set a firm course with fixed and ambitious price policy.

We are being realistic, not sarcastic. We've seen cases where some printers, who didn't know the cost of operation for a fairly good-sized two-color press, to all out and buy a four-color press of even larger size! Not are all these cases just among the smaller printers either.

I have yet to find anyone who will argue the case that costs are not fact and pricing is not policy. Yet we can see time and again cases of setting policy without the facts to back up decisions.

Have you heard this old complaint: "When my volume declines just a little bit, my cost accountant shows me how my costs have sky-rocketed!" For every time I have heard that, there are surely 20 others thinking the same thing and I don't even know them! And what makes it more difficult is that some of these executives are sitting upon pretty good cost systems. All kinds of detailed cost data, completed job tickets, time cards and accurate payroll distributions and what not. It must be that "what not" factor that is so distracting in our pricing set-up when we establish policy.

The problem is not so much *setting policy* for prices—although that is a goodly part of it—as it is getting the proper allocations of cost as a firm, factual base upon which to make policy decisions.

In our industry today, a full 80 percent of all printing firms are making a whole lot less in profit dollars than are the leader firms. With this latter group, profit dollars amount to about three times that of the remainder of the pack.

When you flip the coin of costs, you'll see that the other side is price. The thin-milled edges are like the profit portion . . . very thin at times with some coins. If we examine further the details of the profit leader given as an example in Exhibit 1, we'll see what facts are known and therefore controllable:

Materials	$855,100
Direct labor input & depreciation	710,300
Unknown or indirect costs:	
Indirect labor & supervision	164,100
Other fixed costs, taxes, etc.	62,900
Variable supplies & expenses	130,300
G & A and selling costs	375,200
Total indirect	$732,500

Now what makes this become the "what not" factor of costing is when you consider Value Added, which is sales value of production less direct materials. For this profit leader profile firm it is:

Total costs (all inclusive) at	$1,442,800
Plus Profit (at 11.6%)	302,100
(This item arrived at by proper Markup on Cost!)	
Total value added	1,744,900
Add back material	855,100
Sales value of production	$2,600,000

Fairly simple up to this point. But here is the staggering fact that much of management will not or cannot believe: Out of this total cost area, the "what not" factor is 50.8 percent, while the known and controllable factor is 49.2 percent—and this with the profit leaders. It is larger with the marginal operators.

Exhibit 1

Profit Leader Firm Profile
Base Years 1971-72 and 1973

Sales Value of Production	$2,600,000	100%
Materials Used:		
Paper	529,300	20.4
Other Outside Materials & Services	325,800	12.5
Total Materials Used	855,100	32.9
Factory Payroll:		
Direct Labor	570,200	21.9
Fringes & Payroll Taxes[1]	69,400	2.7
Total Direct Labor	639,600	24.6
Indirect Labor & Supervision	146,200	5.6
Fringes & Payroll Taxes	17,900	.7
Total Indirect & Supervision	164,100	6.3
Total Factory Payroll	803,700	30.9
Fixed Factory Expenses		
Depreciation	70,700	2.7
Other Fixed Factory Expenses	62,900	2.4
Total Fixed Factory Expenses	133,600	5.1
Variable Factory Expenses	130,000	5.0
Total Factory Costs (less Materials)	1,067,600	41.1
General Administrative	188,500	7.2
Selling Expenses	186,700	7.2
Total G & A and Sales Expenses	375,200	14.4
Total Costs[2]	2,297,900	88.4
Net Operating Profit	$ 302,100	11.6%

1. Does not include vacation nor holiday pay. These are included in the Direct Labor figures, per source data.

2. Total costs on P & L only, the "total costs" used in the calculation for hourly rates do not include any materials of a direct nature. They do include indirect materials and supplies as reflected in the "variable factory expenses."

Based upon the long-term profile of profit leader firms during the three-year period 1971 through 1973. These data represent some 420 plus Profit & Loss Statements and a sales base in excess of 1 billion dollars. The average size firm during this selected data base was $2,586,000, which we have rounded off to $2,600,000 for our example."

All this means only one thing: There had better be a system, a method, a program, a control or *something* if the average owner is to have any hope of establishing a proper base for price policy.

Most printers have paper, ink and labor costs down pat. But these are not, repeat *not*, the basic problem in cost finding. It's that monster called overhead that does us in.

Taking the data from Exhibit 1, we've made a few entries on a job order profit control schedule that could be the answer to where you are and where you are heading profitwise. We took an average big job for this profit leader and costed out some basic factors management needs to know about each and every order.

Then to make matters a bit more revealing, we've projected what would show if we were to have two like-size jobs where there was a *productivity improvement* or *loss* of say ten percent. How would these show up on the profitability analysis?

Exhibit 2 shows this, based upon our knowing the basic information found on the job tickets: direct labor input from all cost centers and material usage. The overhead is applied as allocated according to labor input, the most consistent factor in your business.

The 10-percent productivity improvement or loss based upon the average labor cost carries down to profit with the added effect of additional or less burden (overhead). This of course is theory, but it works on a very practical basis as well.

An individual control sheet can be made on each job, the same as a job ticket, but for executive approval as to what that particular job, with the time and material estimates, will contribute to the annual corporate profit. If there isn't any profit contribution, or fixed costs are not absorbed by the job, why run it? Send it to your favorite competitor!

Basic principles for any price setting policy must:

1. Isolate into pure accounting all factory operations, segregated by account classifications into: (a) material costs, both direct into the end product as well as outside purchased services; (b) labor, both direct and indirect and related fringes, and (c) all other costs, usually called overhead.

2. Further segregate overhead into two sections: (a) fixed, such as depreciation and personal property taxes, and (b) variable costs, such as departmental supplies.

3. Segregate into account classifications both general administrative costs and selling (or Marketing) costs. (Be sure that executive salaries are charged to the proper accounts.)

4. Set targets for profit efforts.

5. Take into account that profit consists of two parts: (a) a return on invested capital, interest, and (b) a return for risk and enterprise effort.

William Whetham back at the turn of the century wrote about "The Recent Development of Physical Science" (1904) and said:

"Beyond the bright searchlights of science,
Out of sight of the windows of sense,
Old riddles still bid us defiance,
Old questions of WHY and of WHENCE."

Jump forward 70 years and with regard to pricing policy, note that it's still a question of the old, old riddles. The reason they are riddles is obvious.

Exhibit 2

Job Order Profit Control Summary Schedule
(all figures to nearest $10)

	Average Job During Past Year	With 10% Productivity Improvement	With 10% Productivity Loss
Sales Value of Order	$10,000	$10,000	$10,000
Less: Direct Materials Outside Purchases	3,290	3,290	3,290
Value Added by our effort	6,710	6,710	6,710
Direct Labor Cost (Job tickets, time cards)	2,460	2,210	2,710
Left for "Overhead" and for Profit	4,250	4,500	4,000
Overhead Allocations based upon Labor Input			
Variable Costs: Labor & Materials	2,020	1,810	2,220
Fixed Costs: Depreciation, Taxes and some labor	1,070	960	1,180
Total Overhead to be Absorbed by this order	3,090	2,770	3,400
Left as Profit/this order	$ 1,160	$ 1,730	$ 600
Profit Percentage on Sales	11.6%	16.3%	6.0%

Combined Profit of three orders, average plus productivity improvement and productivity loss = $3,490 / $30,000 = 11.6%

Chapter 13
Cutting Overhead Costs—Now

"But when people's incomes are lessened,
if they cannot proportionably lessen their outgoings,
they must come to poverty."
—Benjamin Franklin

There was once an old Roman who stated that there wasn't much new in the world, that most of what he read and heard was taken from some previous writing. How right he was. Our few thought-stimulators herein listed are borrowed from others, as well as some personal observations.

Cost-reducing programs are already a part of most management plans, however, in the absence of massive personnel layoffs, savings being realized under most of these plans are usually quite limited. Times of restricted volumes and high inflation hinder this no end.

Some authors have termed this period as one of tax-push inflation plus wage-push inflation. We have found ourselves in the worst of economic cycles—a recession economy with wholesale rising prices of a deep continuing inflation plus a material-shortage push. Washington sure can't solve individual company problems. This is the arena for the tough, hard-nosed manager who faces the cost challenge every working day. He is on the firing line.

The advice to cut overhead filters down from the top. Managers at the various plant, divisional or departmental levels are required to carry out the vague orders to cut. And quite often the savings fail to pay for the efforts put forth.

There are usually two roads to follow: First, trim off the fat (it shouldn't have been allowed to get there in the first place) or, second, get to where you want to go by new roads of more efficient operations, get rid of duplication and overlapping responsibilities and other organizational roadblocks to profit.

We must not forget that sometimes increased volume and better pricing will more than offset a high overhead factor. Because your customers also have cost problems, the best way to increase your sales volume is to show them the way to *better value* for their cost dollar. Their cost dollar is your sales dollar. A better weight paper might save big money for a catalog house. And you will "lock in" a customer who will respect the guy who provides him with the savings in mailing operations.

It's all food for thought.

To achieve a balanced cost position, it is first necesary to integrate all *cost controls*. The prime requisite for this job is talented employees. Assuming that we have them, the next step is to delegate responsibility and with it the necessary authority. The delegation of responsibility is absolutely essential in developing a man's abilities, but responsibility without commensurate authority is frustrating and destroys his initiative.

In the grammar of business, the word "controls" is not the plural of the word "control." Not only do more "controls" not necessarily give more "control"—the two words, in the context of business and industry have different meanings altogether. "Controls" are measurement and information, while "control" means direction. "Controls" pertain to means, "control" to an end. "Controls" deals with facts, that is with historic events. "Control" deals with expectations, that is with the future. "Controls" are analytical and operational, concerned with what was and is. "Control" is concerned with what ought to be, with significance rather than with meaning.

Everyone in an organization must be encouraged to think creatively. Creativity is essential to any business operation. The ability of management to adapt to new or changing conditions and to turn them to advantage demands thinking beyond the established confines of past experience. Indeed, the capacity for creative thinking is one of a business organization's most valuable, even though unmeasurable, assets. The five fundamental steps of the creative process are as follows:

Recognition: sensing and defining the problem;

Preparation: gathering pertinent data;

Incubation: reviewing the data and analyzing them;

Illumination: recognizing the possible solutions and comparing them, and

Verification: testing the selected solution.

Assuming that a company has carefully devised and constructed policies, it is management's responsibility to interpret them constructively and apply them positively. With the proper attitude, each successive level of management can add impetus to the drive to achieve each goal or objective as it presents itself, in much the same manner as a multi-stage rocket makes its way moonward. The old adage, "Nothing succeeds like success," certainly describes the organization that embraces the continuing-improvement philosophy. It applies equally well to increased productivity, cost reduction, accident prevention, equality improvement, and all other constructive programs.

Any work that takes on the task of directing management effort towards cost reduction has got to take on the effect of paperwork in our total system today. And we are paperwork happy from top to bottom. And we'll not even mention the worst monster of all as a profit killer: The good graces of the federal, state and local governments. Please, let's not all gag at once. The echoes could shake up the concrete towers from coast to coast.

Let's keep it at our one firm level. Our firm and our people.

"But you must remember that the cost of paperwork does not bear a constant ratio to an organization's output. It tends rather to rise in accordance with the law of nature to which I have modestly attached my name. One aspect of this law concerns the way in which rewards— salary, prestige—go to the man with the larger number of subordinates." So saith the old prophet, C. Northcote Parkinson.

Now let's put that one little principle to work for us. Future cost reduction will be eased as a continuing problem if, repeat, *if,* we get into the application of the prophet's words when it comes to the selection, training and requirements of . . . the first line foreman.

A company that tells its foremen that the job is human relations but which then promotes the foreman who best does his paperwork, makes it very clear to even the dumbest man in the shop that it wants paperwork rather than human relations. And it will get paperwork.

And with all the "fine paperwork" will come cost and cost and more cost.

Input cost: time to write it up. (1st level)
Input cost: second level review and perhaps approval.
Input cost: write approval and "give" authority to correct an obvious bad situation in cost control and deviation from standard.
Input cost: foreman reads approval and gets the job done.
Input cost: writing, typing, filing, carrying the inter-office correspondence.
Input cost: silly and stupid little office memos up the line to prove that each and every level of management is doing "its job."

Ole C. Northcote also said . . . something about a firm with a head office of 1,000 people being able to generate enough internal memos to completely live thereby. No profit . . . just lots and lots of what the educators call "busy work."

To a lesser degree, we are all—every one of us—troubled by this. A note in passing . . . one mid west printer—a real winner—with profits beyond the 20% mark . . . has a minimum of top management personnel writing memos. Few files also! It can be done.

"Overhead" is a much used but little understood word. It's a disease that eats away at our profit structure. Often it is out of control because those who create costs are unaware of their impact upon the total corporate profit picture. This lack of knowledge is really unnecessary, and no firm can really afford to "assume" overhead costs are ever at satisfactory levels. Continuing drives must be made to sharply reduce overhead costs that are either unacceptable or beyond effective control.

A person who has tried to reduce costs quickly may be impressed by the wide variety of cost-reduction opportunities and the apparently large number of circumstances which made the cost reductions possible. In fact, however, results are achieved by applying a relatively few techniques to a wide variety of situations. These techniques, of course, are not necessarily those which he would have applied if he had more time. Many effective cost-reduction techniques require extensive study; when time is of the essence, no apology is necessary for not using them.

Don't just "cut cost"—why not "replace expenditures"?

1. Enlist the cooperation of all levels of management through frank and open discussions of short- and long-term objectives. Review the best techniques; you must get company-wide participation, for it is immeasurably better than that of only top management and specialized staff groups.

2. Examine the company policy where much of any expenditure is determined by management's standard of excellence. See if a lower standard with fewer frills will suffice. For example, by cutting back, by eliminating, by stretching out, or by restricting participation, will it work?

3. Make quick, rough "rule-of-thumb" checks to determine that all units—plants, direct and indirect departments, selling and administrative departments, or even smaller units, especially those whose work should vary with volume, have made reasonably proportionate reductions in time or in the number of their employees. Bring pressure to bear upon those units which have not so reduced their staffs, or cut time.

4. Reassign or reschedule the reduced workloads to eliminate slack and develop a full workload for the remaining units or individuals.

5. Investigate the practicality of purchasing or renting services now self-provided. Check out all the trade shops in type, prep, and bindery. Are our departments and/or divisions really paying their way and providing a *good* return of investment dollar?

6. Combine and consolidate separate units—plants, sales offices, warehouses, departments, and the like—to reduce equipment, work force and supervisory requirements.

7. Check out this possibility: Ascertain whether the cost of goods and services (including the company's own executive talent) can and should be renegotiated with important vendors, with officers and key employees, with landlords, even with distributors, etc.

8. Most important one of all! Implement cost reduction or profit improvement ideas and programs which were previously deferred because business was good or the "climate" was not right. And get *all* employees' participation in this one!

Now that we have said a few words about what should be done, it is only fitting that we cover the basic errors in most cost-reduction plans. There are as many as there are finger prints, each slightly modified by the firm and manager that produce and feed them. They come in all sizes and shapes. We've not time to digest the whole group so here are the big half dozen:

The broad scope of cost-cutting pitfalls:

Payroll Slashing

Nit Picking, ¢ Savings, Not $

Replace Purpose With Panic

Neglect The Craftsman

Cut The Capital Budget

Weaken Your Management Team

That is a shotgun approach directed at the error problem, so let's view these one at a time.

1. Payroll Slashing—This wide-based, across-the-board cutting of personnel to quickly establish a lower wage cost or departmental salary cost, often is done at the expense of trained craftsmen and valuable, knowledgeable clerical people. This is the most dramatic, rapid way to meet percentage or dollar cuts imposed upon departments by chief executives, the type of orders that come down with . . . "Cut at least 10% off the payrolls at once!" Such idiotic commands should never have to be made under normal economic swings of the business cycle or even in such times as these. Any proper evaluation of marketing conditions, back orders, and feedback from knowledgeable sales management should have prepared for slower, *deliberate*, realistic wage and salary trimming. This can be done with less panic and better results for the future as well as for the immediate "tight period."

2. Nit Picking savings in ¢ and not in $—The real management function of evaluation and decision based upon well-informed middle and lower levels of management puts the pressure where it's essential and forgets where it isn't. The old saw . . . look out for the pennies and the dollars will watch out for themselves . . . (to paraphrase it my way) . . . is not at stake here, for this is the second function of lower management—to control all these normal little continuing costs. What we're saying here is that the improper targets have been selected. Many, many litle misdirected efforts do not equal one large and sometimes *obvious* piece of fat that needs correcting. The obvious may be in the front office!

3. The replacement of purpose with panic—No plans, no targets, no goals . . . just cut and cut and *cut*. Often it is an artery or two that are cut. The corporation can hardly recover from the poor use of a surgeon's knife when smaller pruning shears would have been far more effective. That kind of action moves to kill future corporate growth.

4. Neglect lower level blue collar workers—This is a capital offense with management, yet it is one of the most common. The real cost savings from good methods and systems may well be in the minds of your crafts-men and indirect labor personnel, not necessarily in the mind of the new hot shot MBA or otherwise higher level educated management man. He may well pass by a gem of an idea by a mere sluff-off of a pressman by saying "Don't bother me now, Sam, I'm busy." Sam may never again try to get anyone on the management team to hear out his excellent idea to realign a work station that needs turning into a profit center and not a cost center with an over-hungry overhead appetite, at that.

5. Cut back on the Capital Budget—the old high road for the losers! Almost without exception, the profit leader firms we know continue on with equipment replacement when called for. Not luxury purchases to replace money-making equipment, but when called for . . . even in hard times . . . they *spend money* to *make money*. I have too many case histories in the files to believe otherwise.

6. Weaken Middle Management by the top-level executives' failure to really sell the idea of cost control—and because they push cost reduction to the point of job threat and/or fear of replacement. This, at the panic stage (item 3 above) tends to motivate only by fear. If your first-line foremen and plant supervisory people are going to feel this way, what about the crews and personnel under them? This adds fuel for bad negotia-tions on the next contract go-round or it it's an open shop . . . well, it won't be for long, will it?

That's the half dozen more common failures of any cost-reduction plan. How much better to begin the whole thing off on the right foot and scratch the words "cost reduction" with their negative sound and go for the same end results via the words "profit improvement."

The details can be identical, the elements to be controlled, the same, the plan, goals and targets unchanged and yet . . . even such a simple little thing as a name change may well mean replacing fear with pride. And if words aren't really important in our business, tell it to the next ad man who calls one of your key sales personnel about some name changes with a *Fortune* 500 soap company that is planning a full line ad campaign and name change promotion.

Words do count . . . they are the vehicles upon which our ideas move. And after all, management should be more concerned with ideas than things.

Chapter 14
Why the Mechanics of Pricing are the Mechanics of Profit

The first group of professional printing managers was about to receive their caps and gowns and go forth worlds to conquer! The Duke of Illyria was addressing the class in that fine Graduate School of Printing Economics about the difficulty of proper pricing and stated in his opening remarks:

"Notwithstanding . . . naught enters there, of what validity and pitch soever, but falls into abatement and low price even in a minute! So full of shapes is fancy, that it alone is high-fantastical."

It is a matter of record that following the graduation ceremony this first class took up the cry that still brings joy to buyers and terror to all the competition:

Printers and craftsmen
Rah, Rah, Rah!
Lower prices good.
Lower prices bad.
And estimates fantastic.
Costs very unrealistic.
Higher sales good.
More expenses bad.
Resulting profits nil.
Pity our empty till.
Printers and craftsmen
Rah, Rah, Rah!

Now we know that this whole thing is more than just a wee bit "fantastical," because the Ole Duke is right out of Shakespeare but perhaps it *could* happen. Or did I just hear someone say . . . "It has happened"?

There is no single subject so difficult to get complete understanding upon than the subject of "Pricing." It is difficult enough with a study of the classical economical position where we work only with theory. But leave the classrooms for the concrete jungle and it gets worse—not better!

Let's leave the Bard of Avon for the less solid ground of price theory and practice. But before we do leave, kindly remember that the alternate title of the play *Twelfth Night* happened to be *What You Will,* and that *still* describes the printer's position on pricing! One executive admitted to a group of his peers in a seminar recently that his pricing had all the sophistication of the dart board. Doesn't this actually describe, for the most part, the whole printing industry, except for those few who really know where they are bound for the year-end bottom line and eventual reconciliation with IRS?

Chester R. Wasson of California Western University has had a book on the market some ten years or so. It is called *The Economics of Managerial Decision.* His chapter on pricing calls that subject: "The Tactical Weapon of Competition." In the seller's marketing arsenal it has the fastest fire-power . . . and is ready at the end of the decision-making process . . . no waiting . . . no time delay. It's ready right now!

This is sometimes called Level 3 pricing. And when there are only two other kinds, that sort of puts this tactic of competitive pricing on the bottom of the totem pole. Since a totem pole is but one basic form of revered ancestry symbolism, how fitting it is for our industry where so much depends on the way it has been done for generations. The "follow the old paths" does not apply to our technological advancement, for most management is "gung ho" towards new scanners, new computers, new forms of platemaking and all that goes with it. But the basic principles of pricing are just the same as when grand-dad had that old 1910 letterpress. Our ability for advanced learning had, for the most part, been spent on *how we do it,* not on *what we get for it* and the basic reasons why.

Several very high profit operators in our industry—I mean men who are making it with net before taxes of 15% and better—are, in most cases, businessmen first and printers second. When these men price, it is with Level 1 or what some call the "Basic Price Level." And we must herein state that this really isn't a level of price at all, it is the *decision process* by which prices are computed. How much better to call it Decision Process 1, or 2 or 3, for that is what we are concerned with here.

We need not concern ourselves with Decision Process 2 because we are not an American Greetings or Hallmark type of business, engaged in product line relationships, mass merchandising, the structure of discounts, and all related chain store type problems of distribution. To a certain extent this modus operandi applies to the large metropolitan newspapers as well. These merchandisers are not really dealing with a basic price/selling decision at all, but rather with a buying/price decision by great masses of people.

So for most of us in the printing field, it is either Level 1, the basic process, or that of 3, the price competitive tactics. In theory, the latter is supposed to be temporary and not permanent. But what starts out as a temporary measure often ends up year after year as the main type of price determination used by the firm. And slow disintegration of profit sets in.

Now don't get me wrong. I am aware that sometimes highly profitable firms use the competitive leverage of price cuts to beat competition. We also know that some highly profitable businessmen who run printing plants use this method on the long term as a *strategy* and not a tactic. It is a part of the plan for high year-end profits when all the jobs are added up and the final P & L is turned over to the C.P.A. for validation.

Most of our firms under either process 1 or 3 follow the classification of these simple situations:

1. Bid price opportunities for sales. Order taking, not selling.
2. Price line situations.
3. Uniform price based either on the traditional level of our selling price or the traditional market price.
4. Target pricing, be it from any of the following:
   A. Break-even pricing techniques.
   B. Return on investment or assets of assorted complexity and accounting definition.
   C. Flat percentage profit margin on sales volume.
   D. Profit on value added or conversion of materials to sales value of production.

Almost any industry fits one of the above. We'll not spend any time at all with number five which is called "differentiated pricing." Every time you buy a new car you run headlong into this one. The ultimate price depends not on the cost of the car, or even on what basic model you pick. It depends to a greater extent on what equipment you add to the basic model: AM/FM radio, white wall tires, electric windows, etc. And even on a tie-in basis, what kind of car are you trading in? Pricing is bad enough with the first four. Thank goodness that number five applies to cars more than to products from a four-color 38-inch press.

Bid price situations have created our own particular type of Henny Youngman one-liners . . . "Of course he got the bid—his estimator made the greatest mistake." Need we comment further upon this type of classical loss decision process? Somewhere, sometime, some brave sales manager will lay it on the line . . . "The next guy bringing in a bid . . . is through." But I can hear screams all over . . . business forms sales are built on bids, or our envelope business is *all* bid work, or we have to take bids, and on and on. This kind of thinking keeps the 80% at a level of profits about 20 to 30% of similar size profit leaders. Yes, in business forms, in envelopes, and in webs or sheetfeds. It's a matter of management attitude to know *not how we do it,* but *what we are getting from it.*

Price line is applicable to publishing. A whole mass of soft and hard cover books are on the shelf, at very equal prices. Shop a local drug store—95¢, $1.25, $1.50 and $1.95 are the four basic prices for so-called "paperbacks." Each is usually tied into the heft or thickness of the material between the covers. Each big publisher not only has to dig out the potential best seller, he has to tailor his sales price to that of all the others of similar size and content. This is just a bit of what the mass marketer faces in the stronger buy/price decision process of the man with the dollar to spend. That's more critical than the wise setting of price level by controller, treasurer and top level financial people armed with all sorts of computer printouts of cost data. That in this case is *secondary* . . . as to cost. If the cost is too high, the price cannot be changed because the market won't permit it. Therefore, change the cost.

When price line is your controlling factor you must lean to the production improvement factors. We have to stress production controls, lower quality standards . . . but still get the job done, cut corners here and there. This calls for the stronger engineering approach to the problem. A funny thing is that often most management believes this to be the *only* answer to cost/pricing, when it is not. We'll discuss a very obvious example of this a bit later.

Price line situations are best understood when we look at the classical executive dressed in a Hart Shafner & Marx business suit or one off the rack of the nearest discount house. Size, color and shape may be the same in outward appearance but it's a matter of engineering by the man with the needle. Time and effort of input determine the end price.

Uniform price levels determined by our firm are somewhat the lines of price limitations we place upon ourselves. Historic tradition prevents us from going upward in price, even when the market will take it. Don't laugh, we've seen this happen with printers with presses up to 60-inch size.

Traditionally they priced with about 2 or 3% profit and that is what they got. Tradition builds up over the years. A turnaround to a level of 8% or better will *not be permitted* by your present traditional, lock-in customer list. Get new customers if you want to break the bonds of tradition. Nothing else will work with your old accounts because you have conditioned them so.

Down through the years it has been the flat percentage of profit based upon x dollars of cost that has captured the attention of management. This is the use which we have noted for some five decades as spelled out in the PIA Ratios. It is only within the past ten-year period that much attention has been given to ROI and not to break-even ever! This latter form of profit measurement was touted by Fred V. Gardner of Northwestern University in the old McGraw-Hill Industrial Management series under the title of *Profit Management and Control*. Published in 1955, it is as fresh as tomorrow when facing the multiple problems of pricing. It must be admitted however, that Spencer Tucker in his book *The Break-Even System* published in 1963, did much to bring this form of pricing to the forefront. But be it flat percentage, or break-even, or ROI, we must work with the same base set of accounting data—and there's where the problem gets beyond most of us.

Given any set of accounting data from our industry, if it's honest and broad enough in base, it will reflect the sad fact that only about half of what we do cost-wise has any handle to it. We can only directly identify a mere 50% of the costs. At least this has been true with the profit leadership the past three years, with very minor deviations year by year. If the profit leaders cannot identify more than 50% of their costs, don't anyone try to convince me that the rest of the industry does better.

So far we have not mentioned the classical theories of quantitative concepts, nor the theories of demand or utility. Nor have we covered the theories of various laws such as diminishing returns, short- and long-run curves, monopoly or oligopoly, or general equilibrium. We haven't even touched upon marginal product, or the marginal cost curve, or a whole heap of other long-forgotten classical precepts. These, along with such words as "entrepreneur," are more common to the campus than the actual marketplace. Oh, they may well be at the marketplace hidden from view, but we just don't see them nor recognize that they even exist.

While working on this book we noted inside the cover of one old text our hand-drawn graph with the axis of price and quantity. How simple the demand-and-supply curve was to our understanding when we drew these some time ago. The simplicity of lower price-greater sales and higher price-lesser sales is simplicity in perfection.

But business isn't like that at all now. As Anderson & Schmidt said in their book *Practical Controllership* in the first section on pricing policy: "These ideal conditions are rarely found in practice in companies of any substantial size." Further on they support my argument about the inability to determine costs by their statement: "In most situations it is necessary to recognize the existence of a considerable margin of possible error in the breakdown of costs between nonvariable and variable and to interpret basic cost data in the light of the particular problem presented and the practical solution proposed." And in a way . . . is selling price a solution to cost?

These two C.P.A.s have other words of wisdom for us in the area of pricing: "The most definite help that the controller can give the sales manager is a clear picture as to the breakdown of each product cost into variable manufacturing cost, total manufacturing cost and as far as feasible, the cost to sell and deliver." Now I have been looking at all kinds of hourly costs for the past seven years, and have yet to see any regional or national trade association produce anything that remotely follows the classic "definite" help pattern above. Everything we've seen has been put together contrary to desirable goals.

It is difficult enough for the sales team to get a right fix on prices when given the best of the above. Without it they are going at the problem partially blind. The ideal, of course, is for the sales team to set a profitable price. What happens is this:

Over and over, this man who sets the price will back down from what is considered the goal or ideal profit markup. He will surrender over and over again the net profit and even some of the fixed or variable cost in the hope of getting margin over the cost he can identify, that being usually only direct labor and materials. And once gone, the hope of ever getting a recovery later on is lost. Better prices never materialize and the year-end comes too soon and the profits are gone, never to be recovered.

When we mentioned markup in the few lines above, we meant markup on the value added and not on the materials.

Now let's put some of these words of wisdom from all these great professors and authors together and apply them to a simple series of pricing conditions.

Exhibit 1 shows the summation of costing and pricing on three $10,000 jobs, by our firm *A*, a PIA profit leader *B*, and our favorite local loser *C*. This is what they would have shown in their cost analysis and resulting prices. And these are honest figures. *A* is taken from a regional PIA ratio study of some 25 major $1,000,000-size firms. *B* is from our annual 1974 PIA Ratio Study data relative to profit leaders and *C* is also from the same basic report. In each case only about $5,300 is direct or identifiable cost. Now as we end up the year this way, at 4.1%, 12.7% and about 1.9% (to a high of perhaps 3.5%), we have assumed that these conditions will exist with a single job.

The markup on cost by *A* is 4.27% on total cost. By *B* it is 14.54%, and for *C* it is 1.94%. That means that on a job just like this, *A* has a margin of $410 to play with when it comes to price cutting, and the leader has $1,270, while the also-ran loser has less than a flat $200. Let's move to the example of Exhibit 2. Now we're at the price-cutting stage, for this has suddenly been spelled out as a bid job. Who stands the greatest opportunity to get it? By getting it, I mean with still a bit of profit left in it for the printer who has to run the job.

Study Exhibit 2 very carefully. About half the printers I know still believe in Santa Claus and disbelieve this. Most of the men who fall into the *C* group also believe in that old myth of markup on paper. I have been through this one several times with fairly large groups of printers from New England to the Texas Gulf. Exhibit 3 shows what happens when we go the route of paper markup.

In spite of all the arguments to the contrary, you cannot make it both ways. The local paper merchant and his supplying mill make the profits on paper. Kodak and 3M make the profit on plates and film, and various suppliers make the profit on ink. Printers make their profit on their conversion processes. You can make money justly on typesetting, art, camera, presswork, platemaking, and bindery and finishing. *You do not make it on paper!* If you think you do you are fooling no one but yourself.

There are three factors that do not in and of themselves make a thing right:

1. The length of time a thing has been accepted.
2. The total number of people that believe it.
3. The sincerity of those who believe.

This attitude of incorrect markup has been fostered by excellent craftsmen, by men who could work wonders with plates, ink and paper, but not with *economics*.

The arguments given to me by some, including CPAs, has been that with large paper inventories we have higher warehouse costs. We have added financial costs, we have more paper-handling labor costs. To each of those I nod agreement.

But aren't these costs buried in your operating statements? If they are, *and they should be,* then what you are doing with a markup on paper is attempting to offset costs by a *differentiated price.* A portion of the price goes against just one part of the total cost of the job. This element forced the car manufacturers to the rebate wall. Perhaps it will eventually force some printers out of business. For it is fragmented pricing, not too far afield from the "seat of the pants" method of the traditionalists. It fragments costs, and now fragments prices, which are all too difficult under ideal circumstances.

My final argument is that in *Printing Impressions* of April 1975 International Paper was listed as making 8.6% or $262,600,000 on sales of $3 billion plus. If, with their sharpness of pricing and expert marketing team, they can't make 10%, I doubt very seriously the number of people who tell me that they mark up paper 10%. Then I come to find out that at year-end they only net 3.5%. Who's fooling whom?

If you can move that one firm from 8.6% to a flat 10% profit it would mean at least an additional $41 million. Forget your own little firm. They'll pay you well to get them an additional markup. Become a paper sales consultant.

From a traditional standpoint, paper markups are very firm. They stand like a rock. From an economic view they are like a frozen custard in the Sahara in August.

If we try to be a bit objective about how some of the factors of cost affect the sales price of our production, we'll see that things are not always what they seem to be on the surface. Take, for example, Exhibit 4 where we've compared the one-shift costs for a Harris two-color 38-inch press between company X and company Y. These are regional figures to be sure and as such are the best average costs available. Firm X is in the middle southwest and firm Y in the center of Manhattan. One is open shop and the other is union. These are, of course, 1974 rates of sale and/or wages as then paid.

We compared these costs to the most recent national trade association Blue Book rates (NAPL) and found that we are within hairline agreement as to total cost and the various hourly rates. On either the one- or two-shift basis the variance is almost nil. This is remarkable since neither of us approaches the subject of cost finding in any similar way. They (NAPL) build up from scratch and include even such traditional items as h.p. of motors for energy input and related cost. They build up fringes item by item. In both cases, we use the ratios of relationships within corporate structures.

Our own figures given in the exhibit are within 25 cents on the Y rate and 15 cents on X. These percentage differentials are not worthy of consideration. They are 19/100 of one percent in the X case and 27/100 in the Y firm's rate. Closer you can't get!

Now total dollars of annual cost are greater for such a profit center in the middle southwest—an open shop operation at that. Now we are talking "total cost" here. This comes about by one working a full 40-hour week and the New York firm going by the reduced number of working hours called for under the union contract. This fixes the divisors whereby the final hourly rate is calculated.

But the story of rate differential is not limited to just hourly rate— that's only a small part of the tale. The New York firm is getting a production value of some $49,000 plus from each factory employee, while the same factory employees in the middle south are producing PV of only $35,900, a differential of better than 36%. This is in the products produced or added to the value of inventory.

Exhibit 1

	A	B	C
Normal $10,000 Job with Cost Classification	Regional Firm	National PIA Profit Leader	Just Another Loser Firm
Paper Specified—same Source & Specs	$2,100	$2,100	$2,100
Other Mat'ls. & Trade Shops	1,330	1,240	1,350
Total Mat'l Cost	3,430	3,340	3,450
Factory Payrolls	3,600	3,030	3,580
Factory Expenses			
Fixed	620	500	650
Variable	590	510	630
Total Factory Expenses	1,210	1,010	1,280
Total Factory Cost	8,240	7,380	8,310
Gross Profit	1,760	2,620	1,690
G & A Sales Cost	1,350	1,350	1,500
Net Operating Profit/Job	$ 410	$1,270	$ 190
Profit Rate before Taxes	4.1%	12.7%	1.9%

There is only a 20% differential in hourly rate on a one-shift basis, and 24.9% on two-shift rates. These figures do tie in fairly closely to the wage rates as there is a 30% differential in the first pressman rate and even more with the helper.

Price Cutting or throat cutting?

Price Cutting - Order of the Day and Way of Life

*Again going back to our basic job costing situation
of the $10,000 big job with the three firms
doing the bidding for first place.*

	Average	*Profit Leader*	*Other Loser*
With normal costing Same paper costs			
Operating Profit	$410	$1,270	$ 190
If in order to get the Job we have to: Cut price $600			
( )=Loss	($190)	$ 670	($ 410)
If cut goes to $1,300	($890)	($ 30)	($1,110)

Everybody Loses!

But the profit leader could live with that situation!

The number of normal profit jobs of this $10,000 size to 'make up' for this last loss.	2.2 jobs	—0—	5.8 jobs

This is why:

1. No business forms house can take away jobs
   from Moore Business Forms unless Moore decides
   they will "let it go."
2. No commercial printer will take away jobs
   from R.R. Donnelley & Sons, Chicago.

On a much smaller scale this is what happens with
countless thousands of jobs at each local metropolitan level.

It has to be understood. It's an Economic Law.

Exhibit 3

	A	B	C
Paper cost	$2,100	$2,100	$2,100
Mark-up of 10% (the common term we hear)	210	210	210
Now what has this done to profit?			
It leaves this for Final Net Profit	200	1,060	(20)
Final Job Net Profit	$ 410	$1,270	$ 190

When there is a greater differential between production value and hourly rates we can attribute this to better pricing with the average New York firm (union or open shop). This also speaks for an element of control in the indirect costs as we see the costs below the gross profit line being 32% lower in New York! Now we are speaking of relationships here—that is all that cost finding is. It is the load bearing of indirects by the profit counters that causes the problem.

The final line tells the real story. Here in this paradox, the firm with the higher cost per hour, the mid-Manhattan firm, makes a much greater rate of profit than the lower cost printer in the mid-South. For a $2,000,000-size printer the differential is better than $34,000 *additional* profit dollars. It is all based upon the higher cost levels of wages, rents, and other cost factors. Where does this profit come from? From better, more realistic prices and an overall aggressive management attitude.

Chapter 15
Devil's Advocate:
The Case of Extra Pay
for Extra Profit

"Shouldest thou therefore serve me for nought?
Tell me, what shall thy wages be?"

—Laban to Jacob
Genesis 29:15

At last someone has tried to put a specific measurement upon the excellence of management!, said he, tongue in cheek. In the magazine and periodical printing area, the excellent manager is worth quite a bit more than the fellow who's just good or average! Within the classification mentioned above, when results are measured by *net profit differential*, a team of excellent managers can put a tidy sum of *more than $10,000 each week* into the profit kitty!

Now, such a statement as that should make members of various Boards of Directors sit up and drop cigar ashes in their laps! Yet it is absolutely true! See our Exhibit 1. The profit leader firm in magazine and periodical printing makes $645,000 per year net profit as compared to the low of $123,300 of his non-leadership peer. This is based upon the two having the same volume of business, roughly $5,600,000. The dollar differential amounts to better than $10,000 each and every week—all year long.

Cross over the line into the differences from printing processes and you'll see almost an identical situation between the men who manage the top web offset litho shops and their not-so-well-off peer group. There, the management difference amounts to $9,600+ weekly! (Exhibit 2.)

Now we know we've crossed over lines of numbers when we compare magazine and periodical printing with web offset litho, for there are 38 firms in the first measurement group and 101 in the second, over two and a half times as many giving forth with operational data to evaluate.

Dollar differentials occur in all areas, by size, by end product, by printing process and even by geographic region. There is no single flat out answer for any of it. If there were, we'd have a key to unlocking all the

economic woes of mankind. It's just not that simple. The complexities
of the day-to-day company operations within the confines of a limited (and
often specific) market place cannot even be understood by the largest series of
computers and smartest management men among us.

Nonetheless, we can glean something from trying to view the problem
objectively. In Exhibit 1, we see dollar differences (we've left percentages
because these figures are better understood) that scale down from the
magazine printers with a high of over $10,000 per week going into the
net operating profit—*over and above* what the average firm has as profit.
This is in addition to the average profit. This is excellent management's
contribution.

> What does the difference really represent?
> It is different for each classification.
> It is different for each region.
> It is different for each firm.
> It is even different between divisions
> within the same firm!

You have to know each point of variance from your economic standard
and peer profit leader group before you can improve.

This kind of evaluation shows the need for self-examination by a
whole host of firms. Questions must be asked concerning our attitudes
and overall policies, and *you have to begin some place.*

> Does this difference represent bodies on the payroll?
> Waste materials?
> Too much fixed cost?
> Non-productive equipment?
> Improper pricing?
> Poor overall management?

There is no use trying to avoid the last question. Perhaps, avoidance
of facing up to this reality is what keeps some firms in the very lowest of
the profit groupings. Because we have to be made aware of the fact that
we all operate with the same customers (for the most part), with the same
general equipment, and with the same paper suppliers, and with the same
tax laws, and with the same general managerial principles. No one tries to
be a loser on purpose!

Yet the hard fact of life is that only about 20% of the firms have excellent
managers. The many small decisions that are made all year long are
well beyond the 51% mark of being right for the excellent managers.
Perhaps they hit on as much as 80 to 90% right . . . all the time.

Now we all know that most of us are prone to blame sales volume for most of our difficulties. That old whipping boy does take a lot of unjustified punishment.

To show why sales volume isn't always the "bad guy" it is credited to be, examine our Exhibit 2. Note the closeness in average sales size for commercial printers and the tag and label people. Less than $50,000 separates the two groups in average sales, yet the average tag and label printer is doing so much better profit-wise than his peer group in commercial printing. Almost 30,000 more profit dollars are going to the "average" or lower 80% group. Differentials between both leadership groups is almost nil in dollars or percentages. But the dollar differential between leadership and average lower groups is far greater in commercial printing with a per-week additional profit of $2,400+ going to the better management group. Only some 1,700+ extra profit dollars accrue to better tag and label management, the reason being that the differential between the leadership and the lower group is not so great in tag and label as it is in commercial printing.

Therefore, this greater differential, on sales volume of $1,500,000+ more nearly approaches the greater number of our readership. It also indicates more and more management needs improvement.

There is some very slight indication that the differentials between excellent managers and the others is becoming wider as the years go by.

Exhibit 5 shows the net operating income earned by plants in the $2,000,000 sales value size in the various regions of the U.S. and Canada. While there should be some correlation between executive salaries and profits there doesn't seem to be much in most regions.

The greatest number of sizable printing establishments are in the New York, Chicago and Los Angeles areas, the size of the last regional printer being about half that of the average New York or Chicago firm. You would therefore expect these three to be running first, second and third place in executive compensation.

A listing like this is nowhere near "absolute" as it is made up of many averages and subject to the internal politics of corporate salary schedules, which, in small firms, are not always related to either production ability or profitability, but to a family relationship unconnected with these two "output" economic scales. But nepotism is like incest, it has to be a family matter, and the former may well be throwing some darts into the salary levels somewhere.

We plotted this salary level matter one step further than our exhibit shows. We took New York as the bell cow and measured from their levels. A very interesting pattern developed from it. Chicago levels should have been at the $30,000 level. They were pegged about $900 too high when compared with New York, if we used the profitability factor as the paramount measurement point. Only two other regions were that close to the big two (New York and Chicago) on the basis of profitability. They were New England with upper New York state and the Plains and Mountain states, the former being over by a flat $1,000 and the latter being under by an equal amount.

The balance of the nation comes nowhere near paying executives upon a profitability index. Something else must be the criteria for pay. It sure isn't *profits*! Is it sales volume? Is it numbers of bodies supervised? Does the fact that my dad or father-in-law is president have anything to do with it? Just what is it?

Next closest to the profitability standard was the region of eastern Pennsylvania, Maryland and the District of Columbia. Executives were within the $2,900 mark of being paid on the same level as the two big cities . . . but $2,900 on the *low side*. These men are coming up short on pay for profits!

The greatest differences were found in the two regions that produce high profit levels but do not pay their executives correspondingly. The Pacific West Coast comes up way short of the scale, by almost $19,500 per executive! Canada is not far behind with a short side of $17,500 per man!

We've mentioned seven of these regions so far. Here's a list of where the others stand: West North Central is short in executive pay by some $7,200; South Central also short by $9,800 per man; South Atlantic short by $8,600; East North Central short by $4,800, and Pacific Northwest also comes up short by $4,300.

When you read the list of "short subjects" you are led to the obvious conclusion that your base measurement point is off! And well it might be that Chicago and New York are not the national standard setters *as they should be* but are way overpriced as far as executive salary levels are concerned. In the final analysis, perhaps it is a bit of both—the big city boys are a bit overpaid on the average and the smaller region men under-compensated for similar profit-producing work. But we'll never really know, will we?

An interesting side note upon some of these regions . . . they do have very definite philosophies concerning such matters as prices, profits and sales compensations. The Plains states and Mountain state regions on the whole do not follow the sales compensation practices of the large metro areas at all. The commission levels and compensation packages of the Texas to Colorado people would be revised greatly by the top executives of New York and Chicago. They would not live with such conditions. To prove the

point: on such a sales base as this $2,000,000 we've used, the total
selling expense figure in New York would be about $160,800 with Chicago
very near at $151,600, or off about 5.7% from the New York standard.
Out west in the Dallas to Denver area the sales expenses would be running
about $187,600 for that same sales volume. This latter is off by 16.7%. It
shows up in other ways that also affect profitability. The New York salesman averages some $540,000 plus per salesman each year. Better than
$10,000 each week! The average in Chicago almost matches it with better
than $518,000 on an annual basis which is about $40 per week short of the
$10,000 mark. In the Dallas, Houston, Denver region the average is very
near half that much. It is in the range of $263,000 plus per year or just
beyond $5,000 per week. That's where the *real leverage* is—production of
sales dollars to get profit dollars.

Differences within short distances are sometimes very great. A case in
point is in the midwest—three cities of over a million within 250 miles of each
other, with one being right in the mid-point. The middle city is a long-
term loser . . . at an average of about 3% profit.The two extreme cities have
for years been boosters of the PIA profit leader group, averaging at the
8 + % net level. The overall region is at only 4.28% so the two push up the
average and the mid-city pulls it down. Way down!

Talk with printers in the mid-city and you hear: 1) competition,
2) price cutters, 3) tough times. Just like they had an exclusive on those
fine items of the market place. But these fellows in mid-city have missed
the mark. Never have I heard an objective remark about management.

And that's what it's all about. Superior management in the first two
cities and not-so-superior in mid-city. It's aways been that way. The real
answer is management, management and more management.

These three cities have the same presses, the same paper merchants,
the same unions, the same market place with even some of the same
customers! All three have sharp competition, some price cutting and all share
an equal amount of the present economic woes! This is not a one- or two-year
situation, but extends backwards some seven or eight years. It's long term.

And believe it or not, some even have the same firms! So what's the
answer?

Esprit de corps doesn't begin with the platoon sergeants any more than
profits begin with foremen! With the first, the general beginning point is
with the general or number-one man. That's the very starting point for
profits also. The head of the management team is the one to credit for the
profitability of the firm. It is my firm belief that compensation should be
tied into profitability as an incentive factor, with measurement of improve-

ments and/or failures being directly felt in the paycheck area of the total management team!

But then, some of the profit leaders are already doing this, aren't they? Maybe it is just one added reason why they are where they are. Could be! Sleep on it a while. But above all don't disregard it as fancy . . . there are altogether too many facts to uphold pay for profits. It's one of the oldest systems around. Abused, disregarded, forgotten . . . but it works!

And here's a final thought to dream on.

If our firm could move up to the high profit leader group from the much lower berth where we are now resting, what would it be worth? If we're at $5,000,000 sales (or whatever figure for that matter) and we could move from a net of, say, $150,000 to the levels of $500,000 or $600,000, just what would we pay to get there? What kind of bonus would we give? Would it be in line with an "incentive" for *next year* or would it be an "insult" to producing management's intelligence? And there is a difference, you know. Or *do* you?

Sometimes a bonus really does what it is supposed to do: reward and offer incentive. But we've seen cases where exactly the opposite was the result. The bonus had a dampening effect. This is a hairy problem. You had better know what you're doing. Last year's profits and rewards may have quite a bit to say about what we read on the bottom line come next year.

Exhibit 1

Net Profit Dollar
Differential Profit Leaders over Others
on Per Weekly Basis

Classification	Net Profits on Annual Base Average Sales Size/Class.		Per Week Oprn.
	Profit Leader	*Others*	*Differential*
Commercial and Advertising	$170,700	$ 44,000	$ 2,436
Magazine and Periodical	645,100	123,300	10,035
Book	477,200	181,800	5,680
Business Forms	276,600	113,600	3,135
Tag & Label	175,300	83,300	1,769

Source: Absolute Data Section, Part I. 1974 PIA Ratio Study. By Product Analysis. Covers all firms participating.

Exhibit 2
Profitability by Product Classification and Average Sales: 1974

		Average Sales Value Prod.	Average Firm Profits	Top 20% Profits	Other 80% Profits
648	Commercial & Advertising	$1,573,000	$ 69,300 @4.41%	$170,700 @10.85%	$ 44,000 @2.79%
38	Magazine & Periodicals	5,600,000	234,200 @4.18%	645,100 @11.52%	123,300 @2.20%
28	Book	4,689,000	246,400 @5.25%	477,200 @10.22%	181,800 @3.88%
27	Business Forms	2,211,000	144,400 @6.59%	276,600 @12.51%	113,600 @5.41%
23	Tag & Label	1,622,000	104,300 @6.32%	175,300 @10.81%	83,300 @5.14%
43	Five Other Classifications	NMF	NMF	NMF	NMF
74	Miscellaneous	NMF	NMF	NMF	NMF

Source: 1974 PIA Ratio Study, Absolute Data Section,
based upon 881 profit & loss statements with a combined sales base
of $2.021 billion. The law of 80/20 as indicated
by sales size profits for leader firms and others applied to data base
of product classification. 1974 data is reflective of
1973 operations within the industry.
NMF = No meaningful Data

Exhibit 3
Report on Operational Management: At the Bottom Line
Net Before Federal Taxes: 1974/1973*
By Major Printing Method

Firms	Printing Method	Average Sales Value[1]	Top 20% Profit Leader Net b/f Taxes	Lower 80% Others in this group
101	Web Offset Litho	$6,419,800	$738,900 11.51%	$236,100 3.68%
667	Sheet Fed Litho	1,595,100	172,700 10.83%	55,100 3.45%
40	Sheet Letterpress	927,500	116,500 12.56%	8,400 .91%

* 1973 data, reported via PIA Ratio Study 1974, Absolute Data section.
[1] Includes change in value of inventory + /-.

Exhibit 4
Dollar Differentials and
What Excellent Management Contributes Extra per week

Method	Annual Profit Difference	Extra from Top Management Effort per week:
Web Offset Litho	$502,800	$9,670
Sheet Offset Litho	117,600	2,260
Sheet Letterpress	108,100	2,080

Remember: There is absolutely no substitute for good judgment. And excellent management is the sum total of a lot more right decisions in every area of the business.

Exhibit 5
Net Operating Income per $2,000,000 Sales
Compared to Average Executive Salary Level By Region/Major Cities

Region and Major Metropolitan Areas Listed by Order of Rank of Profit	Net Operating Profit on $2,000,000 S.V.[1]	Executive Salary Level
1. Pacific Southwest Los Angeles, San Diego	$152,000 (6)	$25,200
2. Metropolitan New York and New Jersey	127,400 (1)	37,600
3. West North Central Minneapolis, St. Paul Milwaukee	124,600 (3)	29,600
4. Canada Montreal, Toronto, Vancouver	124,200 (12)	19,200
5. South Central Cincinnati, Memphis, Nashville, St. Louis, New Orleans	114,800 (7)	24,100
6. Eastern Pa., Maryland, D.C. Philadelphia, Baltimore, Washington	105,600 (4)	28,300
7. Southeast Atlantic Miami, Atlanta, Richmond Tampa, St. Pete	102,600 (10/11)	21,700
8. Chicago Region	101,600 (2)	30,900
9. East North Central Detroit, Cleveland, Pittsburgh	96,800 (8)	23,800
10. Pacific Northwest San Francisco, Seattle, Portland	88,000 (10/11)	21,700
11. New England, Upper New York Buffalo, Boston, Hartford, Providence	83,600 (5)	25,700
12. Plains & Mountain States Dallas, Houston, Phoenix, Denver	82,200 (9)	23,300

Source: PIA Ratio Study 1974, Regional Data and Significant Facts Book, Part II.
Note 1: Figures within brackets indicate ranking of salary levels.

Chapter 16
How to Prepare an
Inflation-Proof Budget

"Conduct everything with frugality
and economy, which our circumstances
really now require to be
observed in all our expenses."
—Benjamin Franklin

Let's discuss some basic short cuts available to the printer going through
the agony of preparing the budget. We'll use as our example a shop with
a last-year sales figure of $250,000. The principles given here apply as
well to a large shop, or even a multi-plant operation—principles that don't
change.

Our data for this "average" small printer are taken from the 1973
Printing Industries of America (PIA) Ratio Study. An important point:
We have developed these upon the profile of a profit leader firm. Don't
snicker at the size: this small profit leader does better profit-wise than many
firms three times his size. Is there really any other place for critical standards
of management excellence?

It has been said that "Costs are facts and pricing is policy." We'd like
very much to amend that to read "Both costs and pricing contained
within last year's financial statements are fact—only pricing in the future
is policy."

Every financial statement, being historic in nature is, of course, fact.
It is usually refined, checked and rechecked by independent outside auditors
and presented in brief format for the owners to evaluate results from
operations. Markups show forth clearly in the relationships of costs to selling
prices. Not on the individual product to be sure, but on the sum total of
all sales transactions for the firm. The mark-up stands up and shouts free
and clear, "We were sold at 6 percent or 8 percent," or for many profit
leaders, 12 percent.

The hard fact of this obvious markup is not given credit by the
many who run the race but come up short at year end. By short we mean
at the net profit level of some 2.5 to 3.5 percent, and that's before taxes.

The bulk of all printers fall into this grouping. The lowest grade government bond offers a better return for the invested capital dollar!

Let's take a look at this profit leader firm as it develops a budget guideline for the coming year. Try it if you have been having difficulty in getting an operating budget going. It may just be the guideline you need to prop up a faltering pricing policy or an overactive group of overhead fat that makes motions but adds very little to the productive output of the plant.

Our example, as shown in Exhibit 1, is a three-part building-block technique of rather simple math. We'll go through these steps one at a time. Basically they are:

1. The summary of results for operations 1973 (columns 1 and 2 being percentages and dollars).

2. The first draft for 1974, based upon a flat 20-percent factor in sales.

3. The second draft for 1974, with an additional inflation factor being considered at three varying levels of cost increase (see exhibit for details).

Upon examination of Exhibit 1 we will note that it reads fairly well. It is a very simple design. Many financial statements we've examined in the field are monsters. They tell everything the various taxing agencies wish to know for tax purposes but leave much to be desired from a pure management point of view. Most small- and medium-size concerns have a report prepared by their CPA's that sometimes resembles a schedule taken from some report page of IRS. It is wholly impossible as a management tool. For what the manager really needs, I'd suggest an over-all viewpoint of the standard PIA ratio forms, format and design. They are clear, clean and simple. They are a refinement of better than 50 years' usage by our industry—not by the public accounting profession and the taxing agencies.

Back to our subject. One of the usual questions raised is "How do you arrive at the sales figure for 1974 with varying rates of inflation?" We have used as inflation figures the following:

Paper—up 6 percent, all lines.

Outside purchased services and press supplies—up 6 percent.

Factory payrolls, wages and fringes— up 7.5 percent combined.

Fixed factory expenses—up 4 percent (new leases and depreciation costs).

Factory variables—up 6 percent across the board.

Administrative costs—up 6 percent.

Sales costs—up 6 percent.

Now we are not in a debate to defend these price increases as we have literally plucked them out of the air. They are for example purposes only, and we used three different rates to make it a bit more interesting and perhaps nearer to what we face each year on the practical level.

Exhibit 1

Operations for 1973 and First and Second Budget Draft for 1974

	Data from 1973 (Audit)		1st Draft for 1974		2nd Draft for 1974 (Growth + Inflation)
Sales value of product 100.00%		$250,000	+20%	$300,000	$318,950
Materials used:					
Paper 18.43		46,070	same as	55,290	+6%	58,610
Outside purchases & other . 13.86		34,650	last year	41,580	+6	44,070
Total material 32.29		80,720		96,870		102,680*
Factory payroll 28.53		71,330		85,590	+7.5	92,010
Factory expenses:					
Fixed 7.36		18,400		22,080	+4	22,960
Variable 3.94		9,850		11,820	+6	12,530
Total factory expenses 11.30		28,250		33,900		35,490
Total factory cost 72.12		180,300*		216,360*		230,180*
Gross profit 27.88		69,700		83,640		88,770
Administrative cost 9.03		22,570		27,090	+6	28,710
Selling expenses 6.52		16,300		19,560	+6	20,730
Total G & A and sales cost ... 15.55		38,870*		46,650*		49,440*
Operating income (deficit) .. 12.33		30,830		36,990		39,330
Net other income (expenses) .. .45		1,120		1,350		1,430
Net profit (deficit) before taxes 12.78%		$ 31,950		$ 38,340		$ 40,760

* Critical control points (See Exhibit 2).

Going on to Exhibit 2, we have shown only the key lines necessary at this point to figure the new sales volume needed to carry 20-percent growth plus three varying rates of inflationary cost increases. (No productivity improvements are assumed for 1974—production rates will remain the same, standards will not be changed.)

Solving for either X or Y is junior-high-school math. Let's get Y first and X will take care of itself! The difference between total cost after inflation and pure growth total cost is $16,670. Divide (B) or 87.67 into this and you get $18,950 (rounded off to nearest $10, as we've done in all these calculations). Now take the desired profit rate 12.33 percent (C) times the new sales volume and you have $2340 to add to the regular profit of $36,990, for a new profit figure of $39,330. This keeps your profit rate the same as it was in 1973 when it was a healthy 12.33 percent on operations.

The solving for X is a by-product of Y. Take the $18,950, or new sales figure necessary to cover the inflated costs you'll have to absorb, add it to the growth figure and you have $318,950 as a final budget sales figure.

For proof, take the new series of data developed. You know that with mixed rates of inflationary costs the details of the various cost elements will not remain the same but will come down to a final figure that, ratio-wise, should give us the same rate of final net operating profit as we had last year. (See Exhibit 3.)

These are the principles. Don't knock them unless you've tried them. We just completed a detailed cost analysis for one profit leader firm (he is doing better than 12.33 percent above, and in the multi-million dollars of sales.)

Exhibit 2

Sales Value $250,000	+20%	=	$300,000(A) +	X% =	X
Factory Cost 180,300	@72.12%=		216,360	up to	= $230,180
G & A and Sales Cost.. 38,870	@15.55%=		46,650	up to	= 49,440
Total Cost 219,170	@87.67%	(B)	263,010	up to	= $279,620
Net operating income .$ 30,830	@12.33%	(C)	$ 36,990	up to	= Y

Exhibit 3

Sales value $318,950		
Factory cost 230,180	@ 15.50% vs. 15.55% for 1973	
G & A and sales cost 49,440	@ 72.16% vs. 72.12% for 1973	
Total cost 279,620	@ 87.66% same as 1973	
Net operating profit 39,330	@ 12.33% same as 1973	

While the staff was busy costing and preparing for growth column two, the company president was figuring far ahead on column three with the added variable of what happens when the new six-color press is delivered.

He was not so much concerned by rates to be calculated for that press as he was about what leverage they would give him in other cost centers. Of such cogitations are profit leader bank accounts made!

Now back to our business of fact and policy regarding prices. It is an obvious fact of last year's operations that our average markup on total cost was 12.33 percent. (Note that we are not into a situation where we'll discuss how it got to be 12.33 percent—just recognize it for what it is.)

Now this particular printer might have added 10-percent markup for paper as some do. If that be really true, then he had only 10.49 percent net operating profit from his conversion costs. (Or am I losing a few at this point?)

If he knowingly can get a 10-percent full markup of profit on paper he'd be better off closing his print shop and becoming a full-time consultant to the paper industry, since even the giants there, with all kinds of management talent, can't get that kind of profit from handling, stocking and warehousing paper. How come printers can? Or is it that we muddy up the profit waters by a markup there and, when the time comes for the final moment of truth, our net operating profit is at the 3.5% level or thereabouts? Where did that paper markup go? Or are we just being so sophisticated by the complexity of multiple markups that *we miss sight* of the *simple, clean* net operating profit figure?

It seems strange to me that most of the advocates of the 10-percent markup for paper (to recover cost of warehousing, interest, et al., so we are told) don't even hit the 6-percent net figure! Their markup on paper being 10 percent makes the balance of their operations look very sick indeed. Give it some thought.

Chapter 17
How to Use the
PIA Ratio Study (Men or Boys?)

"A ratio in itself is meaningless.
It becomes significant only when compared
consciously or unconsciously with a standard."
—Professor W.A. Paton
Accountant's Handbook

The writer has long been a solid booster of the PIA Ratio Studies as management tools for guidance and planning. In our industry they just can't be matched. Out of them you can get budget comparisons, peer group analyses, and a host of other valuable data.

The 1974 version of the study is in several sections or parts. We'd like to review the index of Parts I and II with our readers so that more can become knowledgeable as to what is available for their use.

Section I has, after the foreword, a section on the effect of the paper shortage upon printers. This is followed by the important section on directions.

Comments on performance comparison, administrative and selling expenses, payroll per sales employee, gross profit, and costing and pricing, appear in that order.

Details will not be found here but in various sections following. From pages 8 through 17, the Report on Operations covers all the various sale size groupings of firms, including profit leaders, and the total of each size group. Supporting detail schedules from operating statements are included in this section. Here is where the profit leader firm really shines forth.

The balance sheets of the various size groups are detailed on pages 18 through 21. The next seven pages provide some of the most critical information made available: return on investment and the really important one of economic productivity per factory employee. Now you won't find that exact terminology used, but that is what it is. Find it and use it.

For example, we often hear of the high cost of living in the metropolitan New York area. O.K., so what? The data show that sales per factory employee in that area are just over $49,000. Now this is a Value Added figure, material cost has been removed! In the east-north central area the comparable figure is just under $36,000, or a 37-percent differential! So what if the union scale is higher, so is the final net Value Added figure. There is only 1.5-percent difference in the total payrolls as a percentage of sales, with New York just a wee bit higher!

The average payroll per employee in the metropolitan New York area runs a very good $13,500 plus. In the east-north-central area, the figure is a bit less than $10,000 per employee. That differential works out to 35.4 percent, almost in line with the production differential! So who is ahead? Plant investments don't even enter into this picture as they are almost identical, with only a very small $46 per factory employee differential. Yet the return in investment is almost 72 percent higher in the New York metropolitan area than in the mid east-north-central area. Why? Somewhere there are answers!

Data highlights by product and by process as well as by geographic region bring us almost through the book to page 35. The last five pages include material on long-term trends, a cogent piece on "How to Cope with the Severity of the Cost Price Squeeze," and, finally, the absolute data page.

Book II covers all the contents of Book I, but puts it together (by computer) in different fashion. This is the product and process analysis. It covers the following: commercial and advertising printing; financial; magazines and periodicals; books; catalogs and directories; newspapers; tags and labels; packaging, and business forms.

And by process: web offset; sheetfed offset; web letterpress; sheetfed letterpress; flexographic; silk screen, and gravure.

This section has both operating statements and balance sheets for both end products and major printing processes. Following are some nine detailed pages of geographic data, the major market regions, what's what among the profit leaders north, east and south as well as west.

Top this off with the 1974 Capital Expenditure survey and an overview of sales and profits, and there is Book II in a nutshell.

All told, these two books contain some 20,000 to 40,000 bits of information in almost every usable fashion. What always amazes me is the fact that only about 15 percent of the PIA membership makes use of this important management tool. Those who do can get their own personal printouts of comparative data. Almost all firms that we have seen in the Profit Leader group make use of such individual data. They're unbeatable for planning and budget work.

For some firms we have worked with, these data become a part of the basis of their hourly cost budget target. Many compare their hourly cost data with those of like size, like process, like end product, and like market area. How about that! Perhaps this is one reason why they are Profit Leaders.

Certainly they know more than their competition—at least in costs and related financial data. And it is not based upon supposition.

Exhibit 1 is a beginning point for some profit leader firms we know. They keep running budget totals of what their goals are *vs.* what their performance is. And it works!

We've taken the largst group of the whole Ratio Study and from the absolute data section reviewed just an item or two for your objective consideration.

This is the profile of the average Profit Leader firm in the past three years. And as some have taken great care to point out, please remember that all the data are generally six months to a year older than listed. The 1974 Ratio Study contains 1973 data. This exhibit is of the large group; the size of sales classification runs from $1.5 million to $5 million. The majority of printers are not of this size, we know! But this is the largest group available for study. The basis is the most valid. The size of the data base bears the stamp of acceptance by sheer weight of numbers. It represents the sum total of 615 Profit and Loss Statements covering almost $1.6 billion in sales. That should be enough for the most hardened unbeliever.

When averages are quoted, this group last year had a 4.65-percent net profit. Horsefeathers! That's a bit of mass deception. If we pull out the top 20 percent what do you have left? A 3.19-percent profit, or less than the most miserable bank savings accounts!

The long-term data for this group—on a three-year base—indicate that the lower 80 percent of the group had only an average 2.90 percent profit for each year's effort. Incredible!

On the other hand, the profit leaders, during the same periods of tight money, hard selling, slow deliveries, paper shortages, etc., have managed to move up to the 10.97-percent level. This is a dollar profit flow differential of better than $220,000 per year! In just under five years, the difference in profit dollar flow is a flat $1 million!

What really gets me is the simple fact that the firms that seek the help, that are constantly looking for improvement are the profit leaders. There should be some real deep philosophical statement that could apply here, such as the Hughes Hypothesis:

"The law of 20/80 is like the law of gravity. Don't fight it. Admit that 20 percent of the quarterbacks get 80 percent of the touchdown passes.

That 20 percent of soybean farmers get 80 percent of the market. That 20 percent of the alley cats have 80 percent of the kittens and that, above all, 20 percent of the printers make 80 percent of the profit dollars."

The remaining 80 percent of the printers are usually too busy to participate in seminars, workshops, association activities, and even home-made self-help aids. They are too busy overlooking the business. "Overlook" is not to be confused with "oversight" or supervision."

Exhibit 2 shows the starting point for our profit leader firm's Budget Hourly Cost reports on each operational cost center. Of course, these pertain to the large-size profit leaders for the years 1972-1974. In comparing these with the data for 1971-73, we note that there have been some changes. But, for the most part, the profit level has held up pretty well.

Here's an idea for you. Take your last three operational statements and calculate them out to get the long-term base for your firm. Compare them item by item and see where the differences are. You may begin to note the areas where you are strong or weak. At least it will get you started.

Now, for a final thought. Here is what we have noted in the profit leader firms we know first hand. This is what most of them have that the other 80 percent don't have! It's a sort of magic dozen. (See Exhibit 3.) Please note that we did not number them. You rate them as you would like to have them. We'd like to review some of these in depth later.

Exhibit 1
Three-Year Comparison of Profitability and Sales of Large Firms

Sales by:	Three-Year Total Weighted Average	Average for 1974	Average for 1973	Average for 1972
Profit Leader	$2,706,400	$2,838,600	$2,631,800	$2,637,500
Other Firms	2,564,900	2,628,300	2,601,300	2,443,800
Number of:				
Profit Leaders	125	44	41	40
Others	490	191	153	146
Profit Generated by:				
Profit Leader	$ 296,800	$ 299,800	$ 292,700	$ 297,500
Others	74,300	83,800	75,700	60,100
Profit Differential	$ 222,500	$ 216,000	$ 217,000	$ 237,400
Operating Profit Percentages:				
Average for all	4.61%	4.65%	4.67%	4.48%
Profit Leaders	10.97	10.56	11.16	11.28
Others	2.90	3.19	2.91	2.46
Percentage of Firms that are Profit Leaders	20.3	18.7	21.1	21.5

Source: Absolute Data Section, PIA Ratio Study for years indicated

Exhibit 2
Profit Leader Firm Profile: Large Sales Group ($1.5 to $5 Million)
Comparative Profit Leader Firm Profiles—Long-Term Trend

	Three Years 1972-74	Percent	Three Years 1971-73	Percent
Sales Value of Production	$2,700,000	100	$2,600,000	100
Materials Used:				
Paper	544,100	20.2	529,300	20.4
Other Outside Materials &				
Purchased Services	347,800	12.9	325,800	12.5
Total Material Cost	891,900	33.1	855,100	32.9
Factory Payroll	850,500	31.5	803,700	30.9
Factory Expenses				
Fixed Factory Cost	146,300	5.4	133,600	5.1
Variable Expenses & Supplies	134,700	5.0	130,300	5.0
Total Factory Cost	2,023,400	74.9	1,922,700	74.0
General Administration Cost	184,900	6.8	188,500	7.2
Selling Expenses	203,900	7.6	186,700	7.2
Total Cost	2,412,200	89.3	2,297,900	88.4
Net Operating Profit	$ 287,800	10.7	$ 302,100	11.6

These "average" figures, taken from absolute data of the combined PIA Ratios of the years indicated, represent weighted averages for the Profit Leader (top 20 percent) of the firms engaged in these ratio studies. Each comparison represents some 125 P&L statements of this size group and total in excess of $1.5 billion in sales value of production.

Exhibit 3
The Magic Dozen

Good Communications
Purposeful Planning
Best Personnel
Selective Sales
Balanced Management
Cost Controls
Profitable Pricing
Teamwork Spirit
Individual Improvement
Productive Equipment
Competitive Awareness
Customer First

Chapter 18
How to Engineer
Profit Leadership
by Simple Economics

"The Art of Economics consists in looking
not merely at the immediate
but at the longer effects of any act or policy;
it consists in tracing the consequences
of that policy not merely for one group
but for all groups."
—Henry Haxlitt

Years ago, this writer was one of several so-called senior economic engineers working for a national consulting firm. We were really fancy pencil pushers with big erasers, trying to measure and fit into a precise formula the various parts of total cost to manufacture and distribute every kind of product from printed matter to point-of-purchase equipment, from tin cans to extruded metal and a few items in between.

As part of the job function we had to do the following:

1. Define the problem requiring study.

2. Consider and discuss the preliminary alternatives facing us.

3. Get a conservative estimate of the differences between these alternatives, expressed in terms of dollars (the great common denominator), not tin cans, or feet of metal, or anything else.

4. Translate the rough estimate into a finished product, a management-type report with all aspects and potential effects of the alternatives clearly spelled out.

5. Include within the report supportive data on income and cost on a comparative basis within the various operating sections (division, plant or cost center).

6. Calculate the effects the alternatives would have had on previous operations as well as the basic assumptions of the unknown probabilities of the future.

Then, after making a series of recommendations, we were forced to live with the decisions reached and agonize through the next year, month by month, with the client's personnel as we saw the selected alternative take shape and stature.

To make a recommendation is easy. To live with it is a different matter. Every consultant should have to go this route. There would be fewer management reports, a lesser number of recommendations, and a great deal more conservatism in that professional branch of the management sciences. Firms of certified public accountants, of all sizes and shapes, should not be excluded.

Now let's do a bit of economic engineering with a very limited amount of data: two firms in the same general area with the same overall labor force and identical equipment profile. One is a profit leader, and the second is not. Both take part in the PIA ratio study and are regarded as leading companies in the printing industry.

	Profit Leader	Other Firm
Sales	$2,400,000	$2,400,000
Fixed cost (at a realistic level)	500,000	500,000
Variable cost	1,600,000	1,800,000
Profit before taxes	300,000	100,000

We have plotted each out in Exhibit 1. In the past we have used just the formula; this time a visual aid should help us.

You will note that a time frame has been added to the economic factors of the sales curve and the break-even points. When the latter two elements link up, the profit dollars begin to roll in. It doesn't take much imagination to figure what great differences in price levels can occur after the profit leader firm reaches the break-even point.

The Profit Volume Ratio

$$P/V = \frac{Fixed\ Cost\ +\ Profit}{Sales\ Value\ of\ Production}$$

	Profit Leader	Other Firm
$P/V = \dfrac{F/C+P}{S/V} =$	$\dfrac{500+300}{2,400}$	$\dfrac{500+100}{2,400}$

Profit Volume Ratio = 33.3   25

Exhibit 1

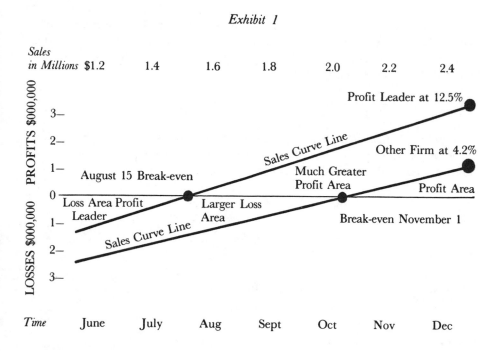

Actually, profit volume ratio is another name for the marginal income ratio. Now we've switched into a wee bit of economics again. Simply stated, it is the percentage of the sales dollar that must be available for covering the fixed cost as well as the profit. It is quite easy to calculate, as all that is required is to subtract from the sales dollar all of its variable costs. In the above cases, the profit leader has a 66.7-percent variable cost factor, and the other firm has a 75-percent level of variable costs.

The marginal income ratio is really a complementary figure, and it can be considered constant (in ratio format) within most reasonable ranges for determinations and calculations used in preparing budgets. The consistency of some of the ratios developed from within a firm's operating financial data varies no more than your body temperature does over the period of a year, or 20.

When you know your marginal income ratio then you can be quite sure what any given block of business will do to the marginal balance of the firm. Lost chunks of business can also be calculated as to their effects upon operational profits.

113

Another important ratio to bear in mind is that called the margin of safety. This is a yardstick for measuring how much sales volume we must have beyond the break-even point. Again, let's work it out for our two member firms. First, the formula:

$$M/S = \frac{\text{Sales—Sales at B/E}}{\text{Sales}}$$

In this context, sales are taken to mean the actual sales value of production. This way we always measure the total operational profit production effectiveness of the company. We are following the standard accounting rules and regulations referred to in annual reports by the CPA's and what has to be reported to the Internal Revenue Service.

Now the two examples (again in hundreds of thousands):

	Profit Leader	Other Firm
M/S =		
$\frac{S/V-S @ B/E}{S/V}$	$\frac{2,400-1,500}{2,400}$	$\frac{2,400-2,000}{2,400}$

Margin of Safety = 37.5   16.7

Now let's put this into words any shop owner can understand. It simply means that the profit leader can drop in sales volume a full 37.5 percent before going into the red. The other firm can only take a loss of 16.7 percent in business before the red ink flows! Think these are the kind of facts you need every day at your fingertips? How much more important they are than the nitty gritty small details that make up a budget or an hourly cost report.

How do we apply the few ratios we have shown here as examples of what management needs on a practical, usable basis for guidelines into the promised land of better profits? And on a day-to-day, or order-by-order basis at that.

Don't laugh. It is being done by some. On each order they know exactly what their profit is and how their long-term goals are being met. Here are just a few uses for these power levers of management:

1. Let's say your fixed costs move upward. The break-even point, of course, moves up also. It takes more sales to recover the greater costs. Simple, so far! Let's see what happens to the profit leader when he ups fixed costs by, say, an even $100,000.

Here's what happens:

$$P/V = \frac{F/C+P}{S/V} \text{ or } \frac{\begin{array}{c}500,000\\+100,000\end{array} + 200,000}{2,400,000}$$

$P/V = 33.3$

The P/V hasn't changed in its ratio but has by dollar amount—the identical dollar amount that the profit has dropped. Therefore, the marginal income ratio hasn't changed either.

2. However, a change in the total sales value of production will not only change the break-even point, it will also change the P/V or marginal income ratio.

3. A change in variable costs acts on the marginal income ratio and break-even in the same way a change in sales does. Both are directly affected.

4. This is a basic rule that is often ignored by some members of management. It becomes very, very important once break-even is passed (we assume that there is a high marginal income ratio.)

What happens then is this: large profits accrue to the firm from comparatively small increases in sales volume. But, by the same token, when the marginal income is low or very small, it takes a considerable increase in sales levels to have much of an effect on profits. Why not grab a pencil and paper and work out a few sample problems to get the hang of what this can mean to your business?

We could go on and on as to just what points can be made relating to the marginal safety ratio also. But perhaps we've already lost some of the readers. A very sharp equipment salesman once said to me, "On that one you lost me." How sad. It is not our intent to lose anyone. For what we are putting forth here is so basically simple it should have been mastered years ago by every plant manager and owner of firms, both large and small.

The rewards that may accrue to readers we haven't lost can be staggering. We have examined the International Business Forms Industries ratios for 1973 (data from 1972) and, to prove a point, let's look at what has happened as a result of some keen management effort.

We'll offer the very simplest data here for your consideration. And like much we have presented, we hope it awakens some to the fallacy of the argument that sales volume is always the answer to our problems of profit. Read the exhibit. No, don't read it—study it instead.

Exhibit 2
Medium Size Business Forms Printers
$1,000,000 to $2,000,000 Size Range
IBFI 1972 Data from the 1972-73 Ratio Study

Number of firms	Totals	Averages	Percentages
33 This size	$59,342,355 sales	$1,798,253	
	2,074,725 income	62,870	3.50% net
8 Profit Leaders	11,456,179 sales	1,432,022	
	1,356,434 income	169,554	11.84% net
25 Other Firms	47,886,176 sales	1,915,447	
	718,291 income	28,732	1.5 % net

Here are some economic facts to consider about all size profit leaders in this IBFI ratio study:

The top profit leader firm paid more payroll dollars per employee, by some $462 per employee per year, or 4.4 percent more.

The same profit leader firm pays the factory employee an average of $257 more per year or 2.7 percent.

It is in the administrative area that the great difference is noted. The profit leaders pay some $3527 more per man per year than the other firms. That is an astounding 40.3 percent more. But you get what you pay for. Sharp accountants, better than average file people, extra bright controllers, money-wise managers of all kinds. And it pays for itself ten times over.

But that's stretching it a bit. Perhaps 5.9 times is closer to the truth. You can bank on it. The profit leaders do.

The profit leaders pay far less for their sales than do the other firms. The average profit leader salesman is paid $13,958, or 7.5 percent less than salesmen for the others. But isn't that indicative of some economic engineering? Paying high sales commissions for very marginal 1.5-percent business doesn't make much sense, does it? Doesn't make many dollars either!

Above all, don't forget that these profit leader firms have a full 25 percent less sales than the others and yet 50 percent more total profit dollars. And in the final analysis that is just what economic engineering is all about.

In order to get into the profit leader pack far ahead of the others who run the race, management must carefully analyze its own situation and then adapt to it the principles of economic engineering. It doesn't matter too much whether they do it themselves, their staff does it, or an outsider is hired to do the job. The important point is to get with it fast. Any delay in the hectic economic chaos which inflation has produced can spell the difference between good profits, fair returns and perhaps even survival! Think about it.

During the past year the wholesale price index of 22 basic commodities rose a phenomenal 32.9 percent. Are you ready to cope with what this indicator tells you are cost and price level changes? So get with it! You really don't have much choice, do you?

Chapter 19
Solving the Problem of
Pricing for Profit

"The real price of everything,
what everything really costs
to the man who wants to acquire it,
is the toil and trouble of acquiring it."

—Adam Smith
Wealth of Nations

Contrariwise," continued Tweedledee, "if it was so, it might be; and if it were so, it would be; but it isn't, it ain't. That's logic."

We need much more than pure logic when it comes to pricing policy. In some ways it is like deciding whether to buy this or that press. Logic and reason are only a part of the answer.

People are motivated to buy for one of many reasons. The Direct Mail Advertising Association published a list on which "to make money" was first. No. 11 was "sexual attraction" (seen the car ads lately?), and at the end was "to avoid trouble." These are all personal psychological reasons. And I don't knock them; I believe them. They reflect why we do things as we do. They have an important place in the bag of the creative seller.

But let's put aside for now the whys and the wherefores of buying a press and consider how to price the jobs coming off any press, old or new.

I have my own ideas as to the motives behind business decisions. There are just three basic reasons: (1) to make or continue a level of profitable operation; (2) to aid the continued growth of the firm; and (3) to make it easier for employees to work (either at the management or craftsman level). The proper policy for an effective level of pricing comes under the first two reasons.

What do the experts say about pricing? Fred W. Hoch, in his book *Estimating Standards for Printers,*[1] says: "The estimated value should be reasonable and should include a suggested fair profit to the printer." No one will argue with that.

Spencer A. Tucker in his book *The Break-Even System,*[2] states this in the chapter on pricing data: "While there are numerous ways for money to flow out of a company (as costs), there is only one way of bringing it in—pricing. Therefore, we may say that pricing is the sole revenue generator in any company."

George J. Stigler, professor of economics at Columbia University, in his classic text *The Theory of Price* [3] says: "The mechanism most often employed by oligopolists in tacit collusion to adapt the price to changing market conditions is price leadership."

Price leadership is something we simply don't have in the printing industry. Unlike United States Steel, for example, no single company sets a price level, with the remaining firms falling in line behind it.

What is it about the printing industry that makes the average profit run so very low? Pricing policy is based upon two general areas of knowledge, one in the area of marketing, the other in the area of costs. Reaching a fair decision goes far beyond the scope of pure mathematics. Critical evaluation, a pinch of supposition, up-front guesswork, product mix and volume are some of the other factors involved. All of these elements must be considered before we even begin to concern ourselves with the competition.

Let's take an example of two medium-size firms, A and B. Both have two color 38" presses, the same labor contract to live with, and both serve the same general region. But their pricing policies and press capabilities are different, although their costs are quite close.

Exhibit 1 shows that they are alike as far as total factory payrolls are concerned. Factory cost dollars are quite different, however. For purposes of example, we've kept the G & A and sales costs identical in dollars so as to make the evaluation more meaningful to those who might be inclined toward a change in price policy.

While total costs differ some $22,000 when we use the correct levels of productivity, they are within a dollar of each other on an hourly cost basis. This is all too common a situation when we measure a new press against one of excessive age.

---

[1] *Fred W. Hoch, "Estimating Standards for Printing."*
[2] *Spencer A. Tucker, "The Break-Even Point! A Tool for Profit Planning" (Englewood Cliffs, N.J.: Prentice-Hall, Inc., 1963).*
[3] *George A. Stigler, "The Theory of Price," 3rd ed. (New York: MacMillan, 1966).*

Exhibit 1
Two Companies with two-color
38" presses
(Two-shift Operation)

	Company A Press 8 Yrs. Old	Company B New Press in '74
Direct labor	$ 52,900	$ 52,900
Fringes & payroll taxes	12,700	12,700
Indirect labor & supervision	16,800	16,800
Total factory labor	82,400	82,400
Depreciation (12.5%)	7,000	17,100
Other fixed costs	6,200	15,200
Variable factory costs	13,300	15,900
Factory cost	108,900	130,600
G & A and sales expenses	26,600	26,600
Total cost	$135,500	$157,200
3,640 Hours Total Productivity level @ 70%	$53.18 Hourly Cost	
Productivity level @ 80%		$53.98 Hourly Cost

Source for ratio data: Profit leader firms in 1971, 1972 and 1973
in the PIA Ratio Studies. Combined for total dollars
of cost and a profit leader firm profile developed for
use above.

Exhibit 2 shows us what happens when we take an overview of the whole cost center from the standpoint of annual performance. This reflects the pricing policy of both firms. One is a 3-percent firm, the other is an aggressive profit leader who helps to pull up the sick averages we see every year in the PIA ratios. And don't think this can't happen. The last three financial statements we've examined stood at 7 percent, 8 percent and 16 percent. They were all out for improvement.

Now look closely at Exhibit 2 to see what will happen if conditions change. Company A is able to cut total labor costs by a full 10 percent, and this drops down to the profit line. It didn't "give away" the savings. Or what if it were able to save a full 10 percent on the cost of materials also?

Then, to top this off, it upped its sales volume a full 10 percent.

Exhibit 2

	Company A	Company B
Total Cost		
(per Exhibit 1)	$135,300	$157,200
Materials cost		
(@ 32% of sales)	66,700	93,200
Net profit (3% vs. 14%)	6,300	40,700
Total sales per press	$208,300	$291,100
Additional profit		
generated by:		
Total labor cost cut 10%		
per Exhibit 1	$ 8,200	
Materials savings of 10%	6,700	
Profit on 10% more sales		
material cost additional		
only	14,200	
Total of three combined	29,100	
Plus original 3% net	6,300	
Combined new net profit	$ 35,400	

These steps all had a healthy effect on net profit. Oh yes. But not nearly as much as the proper pricing policy and mark-up level in the first place.

In spite of these improvements, it still hasn't equalled the profit generated by the 14-percent printer on his two-color 38" press with far greater cost dollars (see Exhibit 1 again).

What goes on here? Is this an example of the expression "Figures don't lie, but liars sure can figure"? Exhibit 3 shows that on a job costing $6500, Company A will sell it for $6700, but Company B will charge $7560. It's all a matter of policy, and it converts into action on the bottom line at year-end.

Exhibit 3

	Company A	Company B
Total cost of job		
to be priced	$6,500	$6,500
Sold for		
(historic average)	6,700	7,560
Profit on job	$ 200	$1,060
Percentage of		
net profit on job	3%	14%

Here's a challenge to all of you who praise and promote the 10-percent markup on paper. On a $6700 job, paper should be about 20.5 percent or $1375. If Company A is a proponent of the 10-percent markup on paper (and most losers are, from what we have seen,) then it has down in its net $137 for buying, stocking, and handling paper. That makes the balance of the profit from conversion, from value added, for all the craftsmanship, etc., a very low and miserable $63.

Yet this is the type of reasoning we have seen over and over again in the printing industry. Not only is marketing knowledge very limited, cost information is almost nil at 80 percent of the printing firms. No wonder the high flyers in the top 20 percent make out like bandits!

We'll only ask you to investigate one possibility. See what a change in pricing policy can do to your bottom line. Maybe you'll wonder why you took so long to get there. Others do it. Why can't you?

Chapter 20
Is the Problem Price Cutting
or Lack of Cost Data?

"Whenever the American economy pauses
to take a long breath,
as it must and should from time to time,
the thoughtless executive
reaches for the panic button."

—Clarence B. Randall
The Myth of the Cost Cutter

Economics relates with equal validity to management of a household as to management of international trade. One might be called microeconomics and the other macroeconomics. While macroeconomics is the term applied to study of fields such as Gross National Product, microeconomics is applied to considerations confined to the individual costs of items such as a nail, a newspaper or a thingamajig. Since newspapers are a part of printing, we'll stick with the micro part of economics and examine some facts concerning this matter of production costs.

A few examples can be cited from actual cases. Let's take one that is an American firm, operating in 1974, as both a commercial printer and a forms manufacturer.

The management of this firm is not satisfied with being just within the boundaries of the profit leaders—they want a 50-percent improvement in profit dollars within the next fiscal year. This is the corporate goal. The additional monies that flow into the profit account are not scheduled to come from an additional sales volume, as they have only moved towards a very conservative 16-percent additonal sales target.

How, then, are they to move up to the highest levels of the profit leaders? Good question, very difficult and very sticky. It would take reams of paper and more space than all the pages of this book to answer the question fully. So we'll try to cram an answer into a few basic principles.

First off, they know exactly where they are today. This applies fully to matters of sales and of costs and, to a more limited degree, they know, the additional market growth they can reasonably count on for this coming year. How many other corporations are really cognizant of one or more of these three crucial success determinants? For them, the data "isn't available," or is misapplied, or is buried in a hopeless mess of accounting data assembled mainly to make tax reporting easier, not to aid management in the day-to-day decisions required to run a business on a pragmatic basis.

Second, our subject firm has set a goal, a target to aim for. Its program isn't a hit-or-miss thing, it is a total, all-out corporate effort to move into the very posh neighborhood of the 12-percent profit leader printers. And, all reasonable variables considered, they'll make it!

In showing why and how they'll make it, we've got a real mishmash of things to consider within the exhibits presented here. They have not been doctored in any way, except to cut down in size. Computers spew out data so quickly that we can miss a whole forest of facts by looking at gobs of tiny leaves. So we trimmed the leaves a bit and hope you can get some closeup views of the forest.

Exhibit 1 shows the cost of operation (on the value added basis) for an eight-station collator used by business forms printers.

In Exhibit 2 we show a 17" rotary six-color press, running with web feed and a one-man crew. Now, when a six-color press runs on one or two colors it is possible that there just might be only one man on the crew. The point is this: Why cost and price for a three-man crew or even a two-man crew when it will be running with just one man? Cost one way and you bid high, cost another way and the job just might be yours. And with a reasonable mark-up for profit. That's what "economic engineering" is all about.

Exhibit 3 is something you might find in any commercial shop today as well as in a host of in-plant shops. It is an IBM Composer, leased by the firm. How does it measure up to the peer group of the profit leader firms? Each of these exhibits shows both the costs within the firm seeking profit improvement as well as that of its peer group, the profit leader at the 12-percent net level.

One final exhibit, 4, shows the various specific areas within each cost center where the *heat* needs to be applied. The reason we selected this mix of equipment is for diversity.

Each area is different in variable and fixed factory costs. Both dollars and ratios are different in the variables and only the ratios are the same in the other fixed costs. Very wide differentials occur between the utilization of supplies and miscellaneous plant expenses, as we can see when we compare the press with the collator. This press cost is 30 percent higher than the peer group's figure for variable costs, while over in the bindery our 8-percent printer is beating the profit leaders by some 20 percent.

However excellent in itself, examination of the Profit and Loss statement and comparison with data on a peer group such as Printing Industries of America's profit leaders (as identified in its Ratio Studies) is only the beginning of profit improvement. I could be the Number One booster of the use of ratios such as those in the PIA study, but I feel they must be recognized as just the beginning-line of the race toward improved profitability.

Exhibit 1
Hamilton Eight-Station Collator

Crew 2: Journeyman and helper
Capitalized at $79,930
Combined hourly rate two men: $11.43
One-Shift Operation:
    Business Forms Application

	8% Printer	*12% Printer*
Direct Labor	$19,796.76	$19,796.76
Fringes & Payroll Taxes	6,432.35	5,953.14
Indirect Labor &		
Supervision	11,724.41	9,710.29
Total Factory Labor	37,953.52	35,460.19
Depreciation	7,993.00	7,993.00
Other Fixed Factory Cost	11,270.13	7,593.35
Variable Factory Costs	5,727.39	6,875.97
Total Factory Cost[1]	62,944.04	57,922.51
General Administrative		
and Sales Cost[2]	11,455.82	13,310.59
Total Costs	$74,399.86	$71,233.10
Budgeted Hourly Costs at		
Factory Cost 80%	$ 45.41	$ 41.79
Total Cost 80%	53.68	51.39

[1] This does not agree in terminology with "Total Factory Cost" as shown on the Profit & Loss Statement. This does not include any Direct Material Cost.
[2] Sales Salaries and Commissions are excluded and Interest Expense is included, as a Cost of Operations.

Exhibit 2
17" Rotary Press, Six-Color

Crew 1 (running as one- or two-color units)
Capitalized at $141,050
Hourly Rate $7.25
One-Shift Operation:
  Business Forms Application

	8% Printer	12% Printer
Direct Labor	$12,557.00	$12,557.00
Fringes & Payroll Taxes	3,966.91	3,776.05
Indirect Labor &		
Supervision	7,386.19	6,159.19
Total Factory Labor	23,910.10	22,492.24
Depreciation	14,105.00	14,105.00
Other Fixed Factory Cost	19,888.05	13,399.75
Variable Factory Costs	9,716.15	6,734.59
General Administrative		
and Sales Cost	12,306.71	13,036.92
Total Costs	$79,926.01	$69,768.50
Budgeted Hourly Costs at		
Factory Cost 80%	$ 48.79	$ 40.93
Total Cost 80%	57.67	50.34

Notes 1 and 2, Exhibit 1 apply
to this data also.

Last year, North American Publishing Co. began a series of manuals, or basic texts in the microeconomical area for such equipment as phototypesetting, platemaking and cameras, all kinds of presses and full bindery lines with all types of equipment, including that of the specialty areas such as business forms.* We have been selected by the publishers to prepare the cost data and put together a meaningful, workable cost guide to production, such as shown in these basic examples. We shall have minor changes in format, because we cannot show within such a study the effect of proper costing on just one firm, as we do in this article. We will, however, base our data upon current union scales and the operating cost profile of the printing profit leader—the 12-percent net man that so many of our industry see only from afar, and get a tail end view at that!

* The first of these, *Handbook of Operating Costs and Specifications for Phototypesetting Equipment,* has been published and is now available for purchase.

Exhibit 3
IBM Composer Unit

Leased Annual Cost $1,992
Hourly Rate $7.38
One-Shift Operation:
  Business Forms Application

	8% Printer	*12% Printer*
Direct Labor	$12,782.16	$12,782.16
Fringes & Payroll Taxes	4,143.10	3,843.76
Indirect Labor &		
Supervision	7,565.59	6,269.63
Total Factory Payroll	24,490.85	22,895.55
Depreciation/Lease Cost	1,992.00	1,922.00
Other Fixed Factory Cost	2,808.72	1,892.40
Variable Factory Costs	3,142.99	3,607.26
Total Factory Costs	32,434.56	30,387.21
General Administrative		
and Sales Costs	5,903.09	6,982.98
Total Costs	$38,337.65	$37,370.19
Budgeted Hourly Costs at		
Factory Cost 80%	$ 23.40	$ 21.92
Total Cost 80%	27.66	26.96

Notes 1 and 2 of Exhibit 1 apply
to this data also.

It is our hope that such cost guidelines will provide a basis for profit improvement for many. It is a foregone fact that there are more printers outside the Printing Industries of America and National Association of Printers & Lithographers than those who are members of these two fine organizations. Most "outsiders" are small printers, usually with 20 employees or less. There is no way to count the in-plant shops in need of proper costing. Our aim is to help the many firms who are not reached by the educational influences of the printing associations—those who cannot lean upon any other source of "inside" help and guidance.

If we are able to help these many thousands of printers solve the problem of evaluating their costs, it just could be that this would have a material effect upon what we so casually call "price cutting." I am firmly convinced that often the problem is *not* price cutting but lack of proper cost information that misguides management into the Never-never land of lower prices and lower profits.

Exhibit 4
Specific Cost Improvement Areas for 8% Profit Leader to 12% Level
Dollars and Percentage of Improvement Needed

	17" 6 Color Press 1 man crew		Hamilton Collator 8 Station Unit 2 man crew		IBM Composer Unit (Leased Equipment)	
Fringes & Payroll Taxes	$ 190.86	4.80%	$ 479.21	7.45%	$ 299.34	7.23%
Indirect Labor & Supervision	1,227.00	16.61%	2,014.12	17.18%	1,295.96	17.13%
Factory Labor	1,417.86	5.93%	2,493.33	6.57%	1,595.30	6.51%
Other Fixed Costs	6,488.30	32.62%	3,676.78	32.62%	916.32	32.62%
Variable Factory Costs	2,981.56	30.69%	(1,148.58)	(20.05%)	(464.27)	(14.77%)
Total Factory Costs (A)	10,887.72	16.10%	5,021.53	7.98%	2,047.35	6.13%
General Administrative and Sales Costs[1]	(730.20)	(5.93%)	(1,854.77)	(16.19%)	(1,079.89)	(18.29%)
All-Inclusive Costs (B)	$10,157.52	12.71%	$3,166.76	4.26%	$ 967.46	2.52%
Budgeted Hourly Costs at 80% only Differentials between 8% and 12% Profit Leader Groups						
Factory Cost only (from A)	$ 7.86	16.11%	3.62	7.97%	1.48	6.32%
All-Inclusive Costs (from B)	7.33	12.71%	2.29	4.27%	.70	2.53%

1—Does not include Sales Salaries and Commissions. Does include Interest Expense, normally shown after Net Profit from Operations line on most Profit and Loss Statements. *Basis:* Actual case histories Business Forms Printers, 1974 data compared to 1973 Profit Leader Base of IBFI Ratio Study 1973.

The differentials between the mid-level 8-percent printer and the 12-percent profit level printer change as the crew changes. We have taken as our example in Exhibit 4 the 17" six-color press that we earlier costed with just one operator. On some runs, under certain conditions, this can be true. And we were requested by the client to cost it out that way. Then we added the normal second man, an assistant or "feeder-operator," then next we added the third man, a general worker who acts as a paper handler. Here's what we find for cost differentials at the total cost level:

17" Six-Color Rotary Press at 80% Productivity
1-man crew . . . . $7.33 higher than the 12% printer, or 12.71%
2-man crew . . . . $8.31 higher than the 12% printer, or 10.68%
3-man crew . . . .$9.09 higher than the 12% printer, or 9.71%

The dollar differentials between crew sizes is different because each additional man added to the crew comes for a slightly lower rate than the man above him. This is normal for most multiple crew applications, be they on presses or on the more sophisticated bindery equipment (except that on bindery equipment the add-ons may be all at one rate, somewhat lower than the set up journeyman).

The important thing to note, however, is the degree of improvement needed for our 8-percent printer to move up to the higher profit levels. On the average, with this equipment, it means an upward move of between 10 and 12 percent.

Chapter 21
The Business Cycle
and Profits

**"Business not well managed
ruins one faster than no business."**

—Benjamin Franklin

More than just once or twice I have heard the expression "It's a jungle" as meaning the total business community within which we all function as suppliers and printers. This "jungle" operates by certain economic laws that are sometimes very grossly misunderstood, if not completely disregarded at times.

We are now in the final year of a full decade of high inflation. One in which we have gone through at least four different phases of some three kinds of inflationary factors: demand-pull, cost-push, controlled demand-pull and now, even a world-wide commodity inflation. We leave aside the little trends such as various forms of credit-crunch.

Demand-pull covered the years 1966 through 1969. The fuel for this period was the huge federal budget deficit that financed the Vietnam War. This deficit occurred while the economy was for the most part in a boom-time period. The demand for goods and services could not be met by even the increase in all forms of income. The demand pushed all prices upward.

This was followed by a two-year period (1970/71) wherein we changed over to a cost-push. Every labor union bargained for maximum wages trying to play catch-up from the old demand-push cycle and the result was a very high rise in consumer prices and the age-old problem of which came first, high prices or high wages?

With the advent of a very weak form of federal controls we slipped back into a controlled demand-push two-year cycle. Then beginning in 1973 we were subjected to a world-wide commodity inflation crisis that began in the oil wells of the Middle East and has extended into the nearly empty bellies of the poorer nations.

During this decade management men in all industries have had their problems, some greater and some lesser than others. We should give a prayer of thanks that we are in as stable an industry as the Graphic Arts. While it is true that the majority of people in this industry are printers, the reason for thanksgiving can be extended to our paper people, other suppliers and trade shops. We've had a consistency of operational return that must be the envy of many.

The fact that there is a consistency does not lessen one bit the need for better management. Perhaps it indicates that in the long haul, printing management has had an average of excellence not found in all industries. And for the most part, it does not depreciate the others—it just gives a bit of recognition long overdue!

In searching for some economic indicators for client use this coming year we have come across some very unusual figures. Many economists view the various stock averages as indicators of general business health or excellence.

Exhibit 1 shows the basic chart lines of the full four business cycles of the past 16 to 17 years. The peaks and valleys are rather dramatic because we are only using the very highs and very lows as points of reference. Most graphs of market data are displayed with tiny lines one after another showing highs, lows and the cross-points of the close. But our purpose here is not the day-to-day or even month-to-month fluctuations of the market but the beginning and close of each market cycle.

Needless to say, the drop from January 1973 to 1974 year-end was the second biggest dollar amount drop in history—as paper losses on Wall Street surpassed the $400 billion mark. The impact from that disaster alone was staggering but added to it was the problem of an ever upward move in the price/wage structure of inflation (the union leaders will like the *price* before *wage* bit I am sure), and some firms will just not be able to see the next two years through. Some plants, marginal during easier periods, will now go under.

A lead *Fortune* editorial in the December 1974 issue under the heading "The Disaster in Productivity" opened with this line: "The U.S. economy is now suffering its worst and most confounding decline in productivity in a generation." We'll have a bit of comment upon the subject of productivity a bit later in the chapter. But there is no getting away from it. Productivity is down. Everywhere!

Exhibit 2 shows the eight ups and downs of the four basic business cycles we've undergone these past 16 years. This covers the period beginning

October 1957 and goes through the end of 1974. We are now just beginning to bottom out of this last bobsled run on the downslide of the market.

Into each upslide and downslide we have inserted the PIA average firm profit figures. They run from a low of 4.78% in 1961 to a high of 6.20% in 1966.

Now business school professors and classical economists can argue all over the lot that these aren't the pure makings of a business cycle. However, since the market place is where the investor's money and his response to the total business climate—plus or minus—makes its mark, "the market" is what we'll use to determine our business cycles.

In point of time reference, each up and down makes a full cycle almost every four years, on the average. Cycle one lasted 45 months, number two took 52 months and the last two have taken 49 months each. As history has usually recorded, the market moves some six to eight months in advance of the whole field of general business.

In our Exhibit 3 we have tried to show that the overall effect on printing operational profits is completely unrelated to the general business cycle and the move of the market up or down. In fact, if we were to be very "pure" in objective thinking we'd be brought to the obvious conclusion that things for printers really are better *when times are tight.*

The combined 16-year average (unweighted) rests at the 5.38% mark, very close to the median figures of 5.32% and 5.44%—half-way between them being only two one-hundredths of a percentage point off! Now this is no quick statistical sluff-off. This represents the "cream" of printing management as the results are shown in some 12 to 13 thousand profit-and-loss statements and cover many billions of sales dollars.

Since our last reported year, 1973 operations disclosed in the 1974 PIA Ratio Study were at 5.47% operating profit, we took the next closest years, 1959 and 1967, to examine a bit of the detail of the profit leaders and the others. This is shown in Exhibit 4. These three years average out to an almost perfect 5.47%. or right on the button for the 1973 year-end figure. Some very interesting observations can be made. For one thing, the differential is becoming greater between the profit leaders and the others. Both the dollars and the percentages are getting further apart.

In 1959, if we figure both profit leaders and the others to have had a million in sales, the average profit leader at 10.48% operating profit would have had $104,800 in profit *vs.* the 3.74% and $37,400 of the others. This is a dollar variance of some $67,400 and a pure percentage difference of 6.74%.

In 1967, as the sales volume moved up to the $1,500,000 level. the profit leaders at 10.77% would have had $161,550 of profit *vs.* 3.75% and $49,400. The difference here is $80,500 and 7.02%. In 1973/74 it was like this . . . on a $2,500,000 level of sales: profit leaders at 10.95% with $273,750 in profits *vs.* 3.22% profits and $80,500 for the others. The difference has now become $193,250 and 7.73%.

If anything, the obvious is that the demarcation lines between the profit leaders and the others is becoming greater. As a percentage factor just how much *more* does the profit leader make? In 1959 it was 180%, in 1967 it was 187% , and last year it was 240% *more profit dollars.*

Again, these are not just one or two bits of data to form some knock-kneed, hair-brained conclusion but a host of real facts. The combined totals of these three test years show 2,598 firms reporting with 520 profit leaders. This also confirms the 80/20 law, as this works out to a near-perfect 20.02% of the firms as profit leaders. How much closer could you get?

Total sales for this test group covering parts of three decades are almost $4 billion (actually $3,992,304,000) of which the others had $3,032,863,000 in sales with profits of $114,882,900 while the 20% of profit leaders had almost as much profit, $103,578,100, on the lower sales of $959,441,200. That should show the staggering affect of what the *well-managed* firm can do . . . in good times or bad. It doesn't make a bit of difference. Quality of management tells!

Some ten years ago or so at a PIA meeting on the West Coast, one speaker gave forth with some very sound advice—it makes just as much sense now as it did then. He stated: "Facing a profit squeeze, highly profitable printers have almost uniformly taken a disciplined, tough-minded approach to cost control and pricing."

Now deep in the jungle of the current market place of business are some laws of survival. Even Kipling wrote about them when he said:

"Now this is the law of the jungle,
As old and as true as the sky;
And the wolf that shall keep it shall prosper,
But the wolf that shall break it shall die."

That gleeful howl you hear off in the distance is from those wolves who have followed the rules of the "prosper." They don't congregate in very great packs: they are usually loners; they can be spotted sneaking off to the bank to deposit their prosperity. They are extremely hard for the other wolves to catch. It has ever been that way!

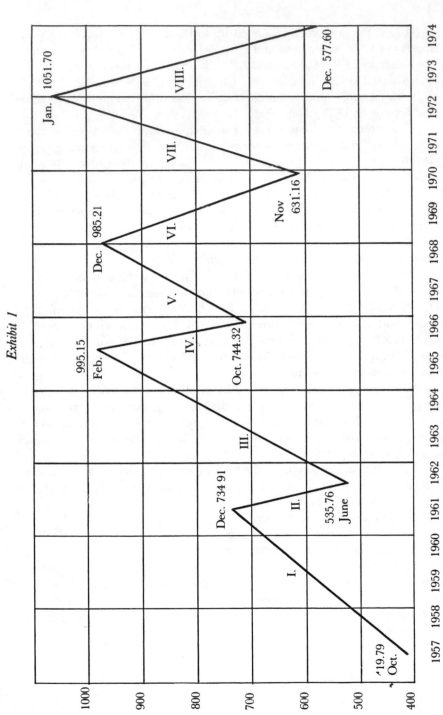

Exhibit 1

Exhibit 2

Cycle Number	Mo. & Year	Begin Lowest	Ending Highest or Lowest	Point Difference	Gain or Loss %	PIA Average Operating Profit	
I.	Oct. 1957	419.79				1958	4.87
	Dec. 1961		734.91			1959	5.44
						1960	5.52
	39 Months up			315.12	75%	1961	4.78
II.	June 1962		535.76	(199.15)	(27%)	1962	5.10
	6 months down						
						1963	5.02
III.	Feb. 1966		995.15			1964	5.76
	44 months up			459.39	86%	1965	6.10
IV.	Oct. 1966		744.32				
	8 months down			(250.83)	(26%)	1966	6.20
V.	Dec. 1968		985.21			1967	5.50
	26 months up			240.89	32%	1968	5.32
VI.	Nov. 1970		631.16			1969	5.66
	23 months down			(354.05)	(36%)	1970	5.27
VII.	Jan. 1973		1051.70				
	26 months up			420.54	67%	1971	4.89
						1972	5.21
VIII.	Dec. 1974		577.60				
	23 months down			(474.10)	(45%)	1973	5.47
						1974	???

Source: Dow-Jones Averages, highest close and lowest close during month listed. PIA Operating Profit, Average Firm per Ratio Studies years indicated.

Average unweighted profit - gain years (11 year average) 5.31%

Average unweighted profit - loss years (5 year average) 5.54%

Gain cycle - averaged 34 months long.

Downward cycle - averaged 15 months. Each cycle, up and down average just over four years.

Exhibit 3
Operating Profit
Average PIA Firm

1961	4.78%	up Market Indicators	
1958	4.87	up	
1971	4.89	up	
1963	5.02	up	
1962	5.10	down	
1972	5.21	up	
1970	5.27	down	
1968	5.32	up	median
1959	5.44	up	median
1973	5.47	down	
1967	5.50	up	
1960	5.52	up	
1969	5.66	down	
1964	5.76	up	
1965	6.10	up	
1966	6.20	down	

Unweighted Averages:
5 down years @ 5.54%
11 up years @ 5.31%
16 year combined @ 5.38%

Profit Leadership for years
1959, 1967 and 1973
see Exhibit 4.

Exhibit 4
Comparative Views of Three Random Years
1973, 1967 and 1959

Number of Firms		Average Sales	Operating Profit	%
1959/60 Total	899	$ 909,500	$ 49,500	5.44%
Profit Leaders	176	$1,170,200	122,700	10.48%
Others	723	846,100	31,700	3.74%
1967/68 Total	818	1,409,900	77,500	5.50%
Profit Leaders	161	1,785,000	192,200	10.77%
Others	657	1,318,000	49,400	3.75%
1973/74	881	2,294,400	125,500	5.47%
Profit Leaders	183	2,547,000	278,900	10.95%
Others	698	2,225,400	71,700	3.22%

Source: Absolute Data Sections of PIA ratios
for 1959, 1967 and 1973.

Chapter 22
Break-Even Points
and Your Firm's Future

"Since management's composite ability
to control jagged segments of time
is mirrored in the break-even point realized,
any forecast should be summarized
in break-even terms."

—Fred V. Gardner
Profit Management and Control

The toughest part of management is controlling change. One item that is
in a constant state of change is the break-even point. This tiny dot
upon a financial management chart carries with it the future of the firm.
Yet, as a tool, it is often overlooked or shrugged off in passing with the
old standby: "Yeah, I know my break-even point. So what?"

Like the Profit-and-Loss statement, this little gem of a mark on the
chart can assist management in more ways than meets the eye. But before
getting into that, let's see first of all why it is that we need a chart or
mathematical formula that tells us when we begin to make a buck. (If
you don't know *where* it is—*when* you cross the line into the profit path—
then you are in need, far more than you know!)

First of all, we must recognize that pure accounting is a very exact
science. Everything must balance out perfectly. Accounts reconciled, bank
balances confirmed, depreciation calculated, taxes accrued and on and
on. All these keep the taxing agencies very pleased, and *sometimes* even
the owners can tell how they made out. But what about the day-to-day
managers of operating departments? Just what do all these accounting
papers tell them?

One of the prime functions of all accounting is to report the *over-all*
sum total of the business—*where* we are and *what* we have done (with the
balance sheet and the Profit-and-Loss statement). But in these instruments
the details of operational costs are generally missing. These are the very items
that line management needs in order to make many little decisions in the

course of running the business—"little" decisions that in sum can mean profit or loss at year-end.

Accounting figures in the top-level reports tend to by-pass the organizational structure of a business and produce figures almost useless to members of the management team below the level of vice president.

Another minus-factor of the data collected and reported by most normal accounting methods is that of "time lag." Weakened profit often results from a drawn-out reporting cycle. We have seen a single accounts payable vendor invoice hold up a whole series of statements several days. We must also consider that interim accounting statements do not always present the picture they *seem to*. For one thing, short-term data can contain distortion factors and it is not always easy to get from them the long-term picture necessary for decision-making.

The last of the factors that "non-accounting" management men sometimes object to are presentation and terminology. Descriptive phrases tend to follow the lines of professionalism within the ranks of accounting and not of management in general. That may foster a tendency for the facts to become fuzzy and distorted. If some inaccuracy in basic estimates and accruals develops, is it any wonder some members of management have a hard time accepting the accounting documents?

We are not being critical of the annual report. This has a dual role of playing the tune to the owners and the taxing agencies. What we are really after is an understandable, between-times reporting system such as some firms have.

Here are a few things they offer:

1. Up-to-date data, with as few "estimates" as possible.

2. Segregation of the cost elements in the reports according to the corporate structure. (If yours is a three-department firm, you should get *cost data* on a *three-part basis*.)

This single consideration is one of the most violated of all management principles in a flat across-the-board view of the printing industry. This we have seen in multi-million size firms as well as in small ones. When one considers this type of management reporting, it is assumed that the figures will reflect the proper "time" element. It is also taken for granted that there will be standards from either past performances or budgetary considerations to measure against.

One of these tools to use in your measurement is that of the break-even point. There are two ways you can determine the break-even point:

by formula or by plotting upon a graph. We'll show both in the examples that follow. First the formula:

$$\text{Break-Even} = \frac{\text{Fixed Costs}}{1 - \dfrac{\text{Variable Costs}}{\text{Sales}}}$$

Let's take a simple set of figures and work the formula through. For purposes of this example we have taken the first of the three departments or divisions of Company A as listed in Exhibit 1. These are different firms—actually operating divisions, but segregated for either tax purposes or for industrial relations reason (open shop or union et al.). This first division has sales of $600,000 with costs in the *fixed* area of $200,000 and *variables* of $310,000, leaving an operational profit before taxes of $90,000. This is the profit leader firm, pushing along at 15-percent net!

This is the way the formula applies:

$$\text{Break-Even} = \frac{\text{Fixed Cost or } \$200,000}{1 - \dfrac{\text{Variable Cost or } \$310,000}{\text{Sales or } \$600,000}}$$

Step 1: divide the 310,000 by the 600,000 to get 51.67 percent.

Step 2: take the 51.67 from 1, yielding 48.33 (express this as a percentage if that helps).

Step 3: divide the 200,000 by .4833 and get $413,820.

Let's round out that figure to the nearest thousand—$414,000—as we have done with each of the three divisions and the total firm in Exhibit 1.

If we examine Exhibit 2 we'll see that the chart expresses in picture format what the formula did with simple math. The latter is easier to understand—at least for me it is. For speed I would use the formula; for better understanding, the graph. Since each takes such very little time, why not use both?

There are several key points to consider when viewing this type of graph. Usually the profit area is so small with most examples that it begins to appear that anyone investing in a marginal business should have his head examined. We used the 15-percent level of profit on purpose—so it would show up on a chart that has to be reduced for reproduction. This exhibit, of course, shows both break-even points, each on the sales line. The fixed costs of each are identical but the variables are not. This type of example was selected to permit showing a marked difference via the graph. The line

X to Z equals the profit generated by division A, while only a portion of that profit (as shown by line X to Y) belongs to division B. In showing these two divisions with identical sales and fixed costs, we have superimposed one on top of the other to simplify graphic display.)

Exhibit 1
Break-Even Analysis by Division and Total

Operating Division	A	B	C	Total
Sales	$600,000	$600,000	$800,000	$2,000,000
Fixed cost	200,000	200,000	200,000	600,000
Variable cost	310,000	376,000	616,000	1,302,000
Profit before taxes	90,000	24,000	(16,000)	98,000
Profit percentage	15%	4%	(2%)	4.9%
Breakeven				
Step 1.	51.67	62.67	77.00	65.10
Step 2.	48.33	37.33	23.00	34.90
Step 3.	$414,000	$536,000	$870,000	$1,719,000
Proof:				
Use Break-Even at step 3.				
Less fixed cost	200,000	200,000	200,000	600,000
Less variable cost				
Step 1 x Step 3 =	214,000	336,000	670,000	1,119,000
Profit/loss	–0–	–0–	–0–	–0–

All figures to nearest thousand.

There are many rules, laws, regulations or principles of economics that govern the movement of these break-even points. Here are a few of the more common ones:

Principle 1: A change in the fixed-cost portion of operations will change break-even, but not marginal profit.

Principle 2: The rate of marginal profit will be affected by changes in variable costs, or in pricing policy, or in failure to meet productivity standards.

Principle 3: If variable costs and fixed costs move in tandem, the effect on break-even is drastic; if they move in opposition (as one increasing while the other decreases), the effect is minimized.

Break-even points and costing principles are important to the printing industry, since almost all functions and production operations within the industry lend themselves to *cost center application*. It is not too difficult to establish the break-even point for the operation of a four-color 38" sheet-fed press, a phototypesetter or a bindery line.

Here are a few end-product uses of this little "fly speck on a graph":

1. Budgets and forecasts. (Yes, it can be used there.)
2. Capital assets. (Why not here also?)
3. Overhead controls. (Is any one of us immune?)
4. As a function of the efficiency level of profits.
5. Policy aids in determination of sales prices. (A real gem!)
6. Structural organizational measurement. (A standard perhaps!)
7. An aid in all types of situations—not the least of which include labor relations and bargaining.
8. A tool for direct costing.
9. Equipment buy or sell decisions. (A big plus here!)
10. An honest way to educate first-line foremen to the problems of costs and sales and profits.
11. Some bonus plans even make use of these dots on a chart.

Exhibit 2
Break-Even Chart Of Operating Divisions A and B

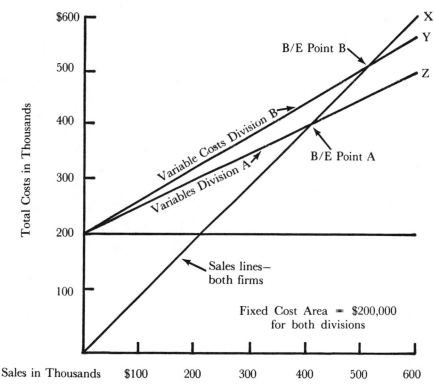

While there are many more uses, we hope we've made our point. In the next chapter we would like to examine the reasons *why break-even points change.* Some are directly under your control and some you can't control at all. But they are the ones you still have to live with, plan for and adjust to. Worth knowing what they are? The profit leaders seem to think so.

In the next chapter we'll also focus upon item No. 9. Let's examine how this much-overlooked numbers tool can aid in making a decision in the most critical area of capitalization: a press, when to sell, buy or trade.

Chapter 23
Calculating the Break-Even Point for a Four-Color Press

"Remember that money is of a prolific generating nature,
money can begat money."

—Benjamin Franklin

When a firm first enters the Never-Never-Land of budgets and cost findings and breakeven, it can become quite an experience. Now, because of staggering cost changes due to inflation, management must know costs *now*—not next month. Next month they will be higher and thus inapplicable.

There has to be a beginning, so let's take a firm for which everything has been working out. It is a profit leader, but lately it has been slipping. The firm is in the top 20 percent of its region, has a good historic set of accounts to work with, and wants to do better. The question boils down to: Where do we begin?

In the following example we have costed out, by devious means, just one of the presses the firm owns: It's a four-color 38" press made by XYZ and installed two years ago. Let's assume that for the past few years financial statements have followed the basic format used for the PIA ratio study. (This is actually where good record-keeping should begin—with timely, consistent financial statements issued with comparative data for measurement, and all data conforming to industry standards.)

When we reach the stage for final determination of the annual cost-and-profit profile of the four-color press, we can solve by the following step-by-step method:

Step 1. Prepare a worksheet showing the seven basic elements of cost and profit as outlined in Exhibit 1. (Column 1 is based upon the old relationship of ratios as they are measured against the sales value of production.)

Step 2. Convert the sales value of production figures to the ratios of value added as in column 2. (This doesn't alter the dollar figures a bit at this point. It is only a means to the end desired, wherein we shall be using a series of combinations, both sales ratios and value added ratios, to arrive at our projected profile figure.)

143

Step 3. From the data supplied by the payroll department, we have determined that the following applies:

Payrolls for the press (Union scale) . . . . $ 70,016
Fringes and payroll taxes 21,072
Total press payroll (2-shift) 91,088
Indirect labor and supervision (Allocated on direct labor) 23,344
Total factory labor for press $114,432

Carry forward to worksheet, rounded off to nearest $10.

Step 4. Factory Expenses come from the equipment depreciation schedule (ten-year straight life) on a press that cost $250,000.

Depreciation $25,000
Other Fixed Costs (allocated) 22,350
Variable Costs (allocated) 45,880
Total Factory Costs $93,230

Many accountants today go to square feet, kw. hrs. and a host of other determination standards. Some of these don't add up to what is shown on the Profit-and-Loss statement. Therefore we stick with the *reasonableness of allocations* by ratios or relationships. Anyone can find fault with the method, but for the most part it works very well when consistently used with good judgment.

Step 5. Combine the value added figures for factory costs less materials. This is actually the factory part of the value added, a mixture of direct cost in both payrolls and expenses as well as variable items in both, all being subject to our allocation methods. These two—46.06 plus 15.11—equal a little better than 61 percent of value added.

Step 6. Divide this into the combined dollar figure we have calculated for the press and it will give us an *approximate* value added figure for the press cost center. This sort of black magic double-shuffle works better than one can imagine in some situations, and this is one of them.

Step 7. Leave the value added concept now, since we have to work back to sales value of output or production and we must next determine both that figure and the cost of materials. Sales relationships are once more in fashion. Our $339,480 of value added computed in Step 6, is now divided by 67.11 (its equal in sales ratio talk) to give us the sales value of production: or $505,860.

Step 8 is where we calculate the *probable usage* of all materials for the press when operating at *that level of sales.* This assumes that we'll use materials in about the same relationship at this cost center as we have for the entire company. A very limited viewpoint, to be sure, but acceptable where you are working without specific data, fully totaled detail cost sheets for jobs, etc.

This is our step-by-step method of ascertaining costs where there are only limited details and a firm must to have a true "beginning place" for cost finding.

As a somewhat inconclusive final proof point, take the projected profit for the four-color unit: $58,620 on sales of $505,860 (about 20 percent of the total company effort) and it comes to 11.59 percent, or right on the button for the whole firm, as per exhibit 2.

To be sure, we have used both sales ratios, and value added ratios, as well as supposition, calculated guess, and a pinch more than just a bit of experience and related good luck. But such things are possible. Sidney Smith, noted author of a century past, said, "Nothing is so fallacious as facts, *except figures*." It's all in how they are put together and viewed. To some they are a complex bunch of jargon, to others they represent reason and guidelines to the future.

Our profile for cost and profit for the four-color press is only part of the way home for a full management tool.

Let's next look at this with the aim of getting to the break-even point via costing. There are few accountants who look upon the nature of fixed cost as actually fixed. The view that the only items of fixed cost would be in the fixed cost section of the Profit-and-Loss statement would make our fixed cost component equal to $47,350 (depreciation plus other fixed items allocated to the press).

We take the more realistic view that some items are "fixed" in *nature* but not in *absolute*. Labor is such an item. (Most owners will part with almost any element except their number one pressman on the four-color press.) A portion of supervision is also of the same "fixed" nature, as are some administrative and sales expenses. Some element in each of these areas is almost always fixed in nature if not in name.

We've taken the following view toward "fixed costs" for determination of breakeven. (See Exhibit 3.)

One might ask "But isn't it better to have your break-even at a lower figure?" The only possible answer is this: "It depends on a lot of things . . . How are you going to treat the variables? How will you control them?" With large equipment it is almost impossible to get by without a very large element of high fixed costs.

Never overlook the obvious!

Exhibit 1

Cost Pattern Determinations Four-Color 38" Press

(Allocations from Annual Profit Statement and Accounting Data)

	(1) Sales Basis	Value Added (2)	4-color Profile	
Sales value of production	100.00%		$505,860	(7)
Materials cost	32.89	=	= 166,380	(8)
Value added	67.11	= 100.00%	= 339,480	(6)
Payrolls	30.91	= 46.06	= 114,430	(3)
Factory expenses	10.14	= 15.11	= 93,230	(4)
Administration + sales	14.47	= 21.56 (5)	= $ 58,620	
Operating Profit	11.59%	= 17.27%	= $ 58,620	

(#) Step-by-step process for determination of cost and profit profile
of single equipment cost center

Exhibit 2

Our Firm Profit Profile 1973

Sales value of		
production	$2,500,000	100.00%
Cost of materials (A)	822,250	32.89
Value added	1,677,750	67.11
Factory payrolls (B)	772,750	30.91
Factory expenses:		
Fixed	128,750	5.15
Variable	124,750	4.99
Total factory		
expenses (C)	253,500	10.14
Factory cost (A+B+C)	1,848,500	73.94
Gross profit	651,500	26.06
Administrative expense	182,250	7.29
Selling expenses	179,500	7.18
Net profit from		
operations	$ 289,750	11.59%

Based upon 464 Profit Leader. Profit & Loss Statements
covering years 1971, 1972 and 1973,
totaling well over 1.2 billion dollars.

These are unweighted.

Source: PIA Ratio Studies years
indicated above.

Exhibit 3

Item under Consideration:	Unrealistic	Realistic
Depreciation	$25,000	$ 25,000
Other fixed costs	22,350	22,350
1st pressman each shift with fringes and taxes		34,600
Allocated supervision and indirect labor		7,800
Allocated administration and selling costs ...		10,250
Totals for breakeven	$47,350	$100,000

These now lend themselves for a comparative break-even, following the old formula:

$$B/E = \frac{\text{Fixed Costs}}{1 - \dfrac{\text{Variable Costs}}{\text{Sales}}}$$

Limited Fixed Cost at an unrealistic level

$$B/E = \frac{47,350}{1 - \dfrac{399,890}{505,860}}$$

$$B/E = \$266,000$$

Expanded Fixed Costs on realistic economic basis

$$B/E = \frac{100,000}{1 - \dfrac{347,240}{505,860}}$$

$$B/E = \$318,900$$

Break-evens also should change every time we alter the sales base, or any of the variables. We have shown a single example where by changing fixed cost you also change the variables. Break-evens, therefore, also change.

Later on, if these two firms under discussion were to meet at an exactly equal profit level at our sales figure of $505,860, from then on the firm with the greater fixed cost portion of total cost would begin accruing profits at the greater level. (See Exhibit 4.)

Change in the sales line has its greatest effect upon break-even. The rule of 80/20 or 20/80 comes into play then, because in our industry almost exactly 20 percent of the firms are making five times as much money—actual profit dollars—as are the other 80 percent. On a sales base slightly smaller than our firm used in this example—at about the $2 million volume mark—20 percent of the printers take home upwards of $245,000 in profits while the big majority, on an almost equal sales base, sneak in a sickly $50,000-a-year profit.

Exhibit 4

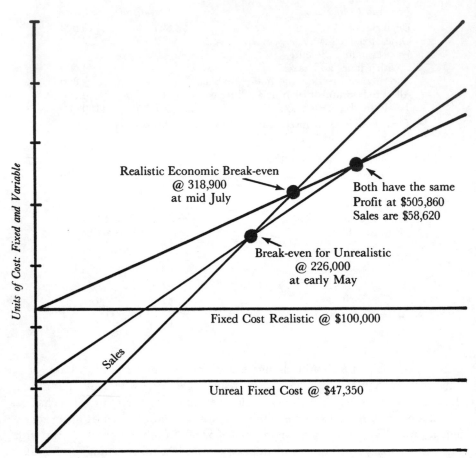

Realistic Economic Break-even
@ 318,900
at mid July

Both have the same
Profit at $505,860
Sales are $58,620

Break-even for Unrealistic
@ 226,000
at early May

Fixed Cost Realistic @ $100,000

Sales

Unreal Fixed Cost @ $47,350

Units of Cost: Fixed and Variable

Units of Production/Sales
Not to scale in order to show variations

Chapter 24
The Magic Dozen
and the Law of 20/80

"For precept must be upon precept,
precept upon precept,
line upon line, line upon line,
here a little and there a little."
—Isaiah 28: 10

Several years ago, speaking to a group of printers on the specific subject of cost control and what is needed for profit improvement, I was puzzled when, at the conclusion of the presentation, one company president kept insisting "But you haven't told us what to do!"

Perhaps he was right. I probably spent too much time in weighing the minute differences within the various ranks of percentages and statistical data that poured out of the PIA studies that summer. I had become lost in a quagmire of shifting and sinking statistical sand. For the future I resolved to spend at least some time on *the principles* of what makes a winner or an also-ran in this matter of profitability.

Recently I found myself under an almost identical set of conditions. Even the subject matter was the same. I tackled "the myth of the cost cutter" for a group of printers on the east coast. Leaving PRINT 74 with all its technical wonders, I was struck again with the power of the truism that *profits* are still generated by *people*, not machines.

Now I am sure that almost anyone can purchase a piece of equipment if he has the capital to do so. He can rent space and produce some end product. He may even be able to sell it. But to operate his business at a fair-to-good profit is something else. From the sum total of all goods and services produced by our industry—from small trade shops in typesetting, or plates or bindery, to the largest, finest companies among us—only a handful really make it as far as good profitability is concerned.

I have been told that I place too much weight for profits upon cost control. I am afraid that my critics are correct. But control of cost does not necessarily mean a pure cut-back, as some would understand it to be. Far from it. The most effective way to cut costs is to *price your product properly*.

Before we get to what really makes a profit leader, let's spend a minute or two with Exhibit 1. It shows a brief overview of the three largest groups of printers participating in the last PIA ratio study. We've shown only two items from their operating statements: sales volume and profit dollars generated on that sales level. But in each case we have segregated the profit leaders from the others.

Exhibit 1

Profit Leaders by Size Groups 1973/1974

Group by Size	Number of Firms	Sales Average	Profits Average	Percent
Sales $250,000 to $500,000				
Non-Profit Leaders	100	$ 370,000	$ 6,000	1.62
Profit Leaders	37	370,000	40,500	10.95
$500,000 to $1,500,000				
Non-Profit Leaders	258	929,100	27,900	3.00
Profit Leaders	55	841,800	98,200	11.67
$1,500,000 to $5,000,000				
Non-Profit Leaders	191	2,628,300	83,800	3.19
Profit Leaders	44	2,838,600	300,000	10.57
Combined three groups				
Non-Profit Leaders	549	1,418,400	43,400	3.06
Profit Leaders	136	1,359,500	147,800	10.87

Source: Absolute Data Section, 1973/74 PIA Ratio Study

Now we did not seek out a series of math data to prove a point—it was just lying there, buried under the host of dollars and other figures on the absolute data page. We didn't stumble over it either. It is only one more link in a long chain of similar statistical evidence that proves some economic and personality laws are almost as valid as gravity!

We threw in personality with economics above because we're back at the main point: people make profits, not machines. The two groups shown in Exhibit 1 have the same craftsmen, same union conditions, same purchasing problems, same kinds of equipment and same customers. They are alike, but they are by no means identical. The differences begin with the personality of the leaders within the profit leader firms. They differ greatly from those of the also-rans. And to make this perfectly clear: the difference is not just a matter of cost control, although that is a part of it.

Combine the three groups in our exhibit and you have 136/685 or 19.85 percent. (How close to 20 percent can you get?) This is a very good proof of the old Law of 20/80, for why do 20 percent of the printers walk off with 80 percent of the total profit dollars? The average firm in the profit leader group makes better than $100,000 *additional profit* on $59,000 *less* sales. How does that grab you? They can't be doing it only on cost cutting.

Well then, what do they do? A good question. We call it the "magic dozen," a series of basic principles that make them winners. It's not too different from the winners in pro football. There are those who run better, tackle better, block better, kick better. These are also the corporate characteristics that grow out of the personality of the leadership within the firm. We've seen them at work over and over again. There is something about being with leaders that rubs off on you. Like measles, winning characteristics are always catching. What are those characteristics? These:

Good Communications. By this we mean with our customers, with our suppliers, and with each other within the firm. Out and in. Up and down. We say what we mean and we mean what we say. Our word is good. Because we have good internal and external communications, we have eliminated much of the wasted efforts of craftsmen, all but eliminated strife among departments and prevented labor problems before they erupted.

Purposeful Planning. This was one theme of the 1974 PIA convention. Nothing new at all. Every profit leader firm we've ever seen has plans for the next year. We could call them tactical operations. The longer five- to ten-year plans (at the president-chairman-board level) are the corporate strategy for survival and growth. They must cover such items as personnel, capital budget, marketing and finance. You will note that two of those items are generally considered to be within the range of administration, usually the weakest part of management of the non-profit groups in any size.

Better Personnel. Thomas Jefferson said, "An executive's greatest task is getting the right man for the right job." In that connection, it is the duty of every good executive to train his replacement so that he, himself, can move up the ladder of corporate responsibility.

Selective Sales. The top 20 percent of your sales effort produces within any firm about 80% of the profit dollars. Likewise, the bottom 20% of your sales produce the bulk of problems and troubles, perhaps 80% of it. To increase your profit, dump the bottom 20%—and replace these losers with profit making sales. This is one magic trick of *profit leaders.*

Balanced Management. Get management zeroed in on all three parts of the corporate body! Sales or marketing, and production and administration. Most firms have the first two well under control. There is a sad lack within number three, but not with the profit leaders. They have all three!

Cost Control. Good cost control means direction. Don't confuse this with controls. I know some shops with controls everywhere, but not the right control. One provides direction. The other is a measuring device. Some managements don't know the difference between the two. Controls can be gadgets and gimmicks. But *control* is ever the better part of management.

Profitable Pricing. This is a natural outgrowth of cost control. It is a directional thing also. Just recently we heard a comment by a 14-percent profit printer (in a region known for tough times and chugging along at about 2 to 3 percent). He remarked that "all I see in the industry today are gutless executives, afraid to price their product properly."

Teamwork. It begins with the general, filters down through his staff and *never, never* begins with the platoon sergeants. If your firm doesn't have it, face the fellow you see when shaving. Ask him why!

Individual Improvement. Motivate your people to self-improvement. Each member of the firm has to get ready for a better tomorrow. Lead the way. Help if you can, but lead, don't push. What kind of mind-provoking and executive-stimulating reading does your first-line foreman do? Ever think that a few bucks spent for *at-home* quality reading, to broaden his viewpoints might held productivity next year? Or help him handle the many personality problems he faces each day? I mean *general* mind-stretching material, not industry-related matter.

Productive Equipment. Get the best, not the least costly. Buy it with an eye to the future, not just the here and now. Spend today to make it tomorrow. Most profit leaders have a good capital budget. They review it constantly. There is no lack of good equipment where fellows with the good net profit operate. And it pays, and pays, and pays.

Competitive Awareness. Keep an eye on your peer group, but don't become overly engrossed in the subject.

Customer First. He is first, last and always. Without him we're dead! In a word, it is *service, service, service.* But above all, don't forget that he has to pay his own way!

An all-out effort to put into action within your firm those Magic Dozen characteristics and you'll see profit improvement you didn't believe possible. It will not happen overnight. The toughest thing to do in any firm is to turn a loser into a profitable operation. But, to survive it has to be done.

Now if you think it impossible, try the easy-pay plan. Do one each month, but make it an all-out, top management effort. Stress that one single quality all month long. Then in future months move on to another subject, not neglecting the previous ones. Profits for 1976 will be somewhat better. But if you have learned the lessons, mastered the principles, the profits for 1977 will really be something to write home about.

Individually these touted characteristics are nothing new. Each has been expounded by this seminar or that convention, by this consultant or that speaker. Wrapped together, they make good common sense. And they will provide the base for the profit leader. If you want entree to that exclusive club, profit leader, you have to pay the price. The price is principle, and that principle will earn you the interest called profit.

Chapter 25
Taxes: They'll Eat You Up
Unless You Plan for Them

"But in this world nothing
can be said to be certain
except death and taxes."

—Benjamin Franklin

Old Ben, the Printer from Philadelphia, said in his letter of July 11, 1765 concerning the Stamp Act: "Idleness and pride tax with a heavier hand than kings and parliaments. If we could get rid of the former, we may easily bear the latter."

Now I wonder what our beloved Ben would have thought of all these taxes now raised upon a people who once rebelled at a few—and they were somewhat small at that! I guess it was really the principle of the matter that counted then.

So what counts now? How do we confront the host of taxes now levied, not by kings and parliaments, but by this representative or that governor, or this senate or that town council or this group of county commissioners? And they, the tax assessors, are not few in numbers. Neither are the taxes now imposed upon an over-burdened public. And the greatest target of all is the small businessman!

Another Revolutionary character, Tom Paine, had these comments to make about war in general in his "Prospects on the Rubicon" written in 1787: "It (war) has but one thing certain, and that is to increase taxes." When one considers that our nation has been involved in war, or some sort of "police action" in two-thirds of the years since the beginning of WW II, it is no wonder that we face such a tax load today. Those old-timers were pretty smart.

Now this is not intended to be a political thesis or anti-establishment letter, so let's switch right now to seeing what we can do about the whole mess of taxes we find ourselves facing as we approach the year end.

The average owner/manager in printing today has had to struggle for survival on a really thin investment package. Cash flow has usually been a problem. It becomes heavier at tax time as our great Uncle extends the ever-lengthening grasp of the IRS.

Today small business owner/managers need to develop skills in financial management which, by rights, should include some form of tax planning. If better than half your earned income has to go for some form of tax dollar—regardless of what it is called—then it would do us all well to plan for parting with as few of our dollars as the law permits. Those who so plan usually retain more of their earned dollars than those who don't.

This type of critical financial management is of greater import to the small businessman than to the multi-size corporate giants. The investment in time will be far less, the possibility of gain greater, percentage-wise.

Basic skills of understanding the balance sheet, profit-and-loss statement, cash-flow projections, statements such as the source and application of funds, and even hourly costs all enter into planning in financial management. Since the most difficult part of small business management is operating with a minimum of working capital, it is most important that we hang on to every bit of it we can. Accounting tools help us along the road to growth and survival.

Now if the owner/manager can't make good use of these tools himself, he must seek outside assistance. This will enable him to detect problems and trouble areas of money control (or the lack of it) before, not *after* the fact!

Taxation should take up some of his long-term planning time. This is vital to any strategy for survival and growth. Foremen and shift super-intendents can't do it, most plant managers give it very little time. This is a job for the man who sits at the head of the table during the executive meetings. In doing this, in middle-size firms and up, he is most often ably assisted by treasurers, controllers, chief accountants or some specialist.

First of all, the owner/manager has to answer some basic questions about himself. Such as:

1. Is he working to build a growth business for his family? Will his children take over at some future date?

2. Is he building the business for future sale and then using the income from that for retirement?

3. Is the business being built for future absentee ownership with full retention of ownership, but with a hired management to run it while he, the owner, goes into retirement?

4. Will he devote part-time effort to future management? Sell off a part to bring in new and younger management?

5. Or isn't there any thought-out reason at all, not for today, but for a few years down the road?

These and similar questions need to be answered first! Now what does this owner/manager face in the way of taxes?

Federal Taxes
Individual Income Tax
Corporate Income Tax
Excise Taxes—Manufacturer
Excise Taxes—Retail
Employment Taxes
Social Security Taxes
Death Taxes (Estate)
Stamp Taxes
Occupational Taxes
Customs

Sale Taxes
Individual Income Taxes
Corporate Income Taxes
Gross Receipts Taxes
Real Property Taxes (Business)
Personal Property Taxes (Business)
Capital Stock Taxes
Business Automobile, Truck Taxes
    (or Fees and Licenses)
Sales Taxes
Death Taxes (Estate)
Foreign-state Business Taxes
State Franchise Taxes
Workmen's Compensation Taxes
State Unemployment Taxes
Incorporation Fees
Employment Taxes

Local Government
Individaul Income Tax
Sales Tax
Gross Receipts Tax
County, City, School District Real Estate Tax
    or Personal Property Taxes
Business Licenses and Fees

Now we all know that from state to state and from city to city
there is wide variation of names and kinds of taxes. But the burden of
filing, even if we pay nothing, is often a time-consuming job. The owner/
manager needs help, for the most part. His need will vary with his own
experience and that of his staff people. Sources for aid may well include
people such as these: Tax attorney, certified public accountants, tax
consulting firms, bankers, libraries, pubic and private trade associations,
tax information services (Commerce Clearing House or Prentice-Hall are
good examples), Internal Revenue Service, state taxing agencies, local
taxing agencies, equipment supplier's legal department.

Any owner/manager who breaks through the $250,000 sales level
should have an outside independent expert in taxation regularly doing his
taxes. His annual audit and year-end report is a natural beginning
point, and the most logical person to do it is the CPA he employs for the
annual audit.

Most owner/managers of small firms wear two hats *very well*. The
hats of sales executive and production executive seem made to measure.
That of administration executive slips a little bit for most, and that of
financial executive isn't even on the rack in many cases. Two hats, yes;
three, maybe; but four hats, almost never!

The smartest thing a small, growing firm can do is get with a really
aggressive tax-conscious CPA firm. Let the men who put together your
annual audit extend their time to include your basic tax reports. They
are real professionals. Not experts in printing but in taxation! That will
be money well spent. You'll often save enough in cash flow and retained
earnings to pay for the audit *and* the preparation of the tax reports. They
are experts in what is called *"tax avoidance."*

Don't confuse this "tax avoidance" with "tax evasion." What's the
difference? About five to ten years difference . . . as a guest at Leavenworth
or some such place.

Management decisions have a direct effect upon the taxes you must
pay at year end. Before getting into them we should consider some basic
ground rules:

1. There are many factors that owners must consider before making
the decisions the firm has to live with. Certain courses of action may
or may not have a direct bearing upon your tax situation. But, that *must*
be considered in all financial matters.

2. The Federal Government does not require us to operate our
businesses so as to be liable for the maximum amount of taxes. Business

decisions can and should be based upon the minimizing of tax effects on our firms.

3. Never, never, never fall into the trap that leads to "tax evasion," or to put it more plainly—never fail to pay taxes due to the various governmental agencies.

4. Lastly, since the entire field of taxation is so very complex, ever changing, and highly technical in nature it would be in the best interest of the firm to entrust the guidance of our ship of enterprise to a professional tax expert and not to trust our own limited knowledge and out-of-date hearsay and/or prejudical opinions.

Exhibit 1
Profit Dollar Ranking Within The Industry 1973
183 Profit Leaders vs. 698 Other Printers

No. Firms	Size Classification	Average Profit Dollars	%	Average Sales Dollars
84	Very Small	$ 3,800	2.2%	$ 165,700
100	Small	6,000	1.6%	370,000
21	Very Small	19,000	12.0%	166,700
258	Medium Small	27,900	3.0%	927,100
37	Small	40,500	10.7%	370,300
191	Medium Large	83,800	3.2%	2,628,300
55	Medium Small	98,200	11.8%	841,800
39	Large	228,200	3.4%	6,728,200
44	Medium Large	300,000	10.6%	2,838,600
26	Very Large	665,400	3.5%	19,261,500
16	Large	887,500	12.4%	7,156,300
10	Very Large	1,700,000	10.4%	16,320,000

Classification Sizes:
Very Small = under $250,000;
Small = $250,000 - $500,000;
Medium Small = $500,000 - $1,500,000;
Medium Large = $1,500,000 - $5,000,000;
Large = $5,000,000 - $10,000,000;
Very Large = Over $10,000,000

(Total sales base more than two billion)
Absolute Data Section PIA Ratios 1974
(base year data from 1973)

If we follow these simple rules when we reach for decisions on such matters, we'll have the advice of the experts:

Inventory: valuation at year-end, a method of computation, year-end purchasing tactics; to buy or not to buy.

Estate and/or Gifts: proper timing and planning for disposition of these often difficult matters.

Accounts Receivable: the effect upon our taxes and cash flow of proper write-offs of bad debts.

Sales: the right tax base and methods of payment.

Wages: the use of employee incentives, stock options, deferred payment plans for executives and sales personnel, pension plans and/or profit sharing, in addition to the normal wage/tax problems.

Assets and Capital Gains and Losses: proper timing of equipment retirements/trades/buy-sell decisions. This goes for mergers and acquisitions also. Should we lease or go with this type of depreciation or that? It will affect cash flow and the buildup of long-term strong assets/capital position.

Executive Compensation: How much shall the owner draw out of the business? (see our list of questions concerning "why are you working?" at the beginning of this chapter.)

All the above are covered somewhere in the Internal Revenue Code. It takes an expert to understand it and to apply it to everyday business decisions. The everyday business decisions will be made easier if the policy has been made *after* a complete discussion with your outside tax expert. He can guide you on such things as:

Investment Tax Credit, that extra bit of first year depreciation to retain additional earnings at current dollars.

How and when to depreciate your recent equipment purchases. When to capitalize, when to expense costs for replacement or repairs and maintenance. Does it extend the life of the equipment or what? Is new equipment treated as used equipment? What happens when we sell or trade a press that is not fully depreciated? How does this affect the cost of the new press? How should we evaluate our tools, cutter knives, parts, etc.? All these need to be placed in the proper tax perspective for minimum taxes and maximum earnings retention.

Most owners are poorly qualified to answer this host of equipment-related questions from the IRS code. Most need help. The latest PIA ratio study indicates that more of us need *financial help* than are willing to admit.

We've taken some data from the Ratio Study's Absolute Data page and refined it to show where the profit leadership really is in our industry.

It is not at *all related to sales effort!* That is an old management myth that refuses to die. It is as if each new generation coming into our industry is infused with the old saw: "More sales are the answer." One thing these ratio studies should have shown since the year one is that this kind of management myth is self-defeating.

Let's look at the most recent record: Exhibit 1.

Now, what is the point in mixing sales and profits with taxes? The point is this: In each and every case where we have been in contact with printers, we have noted one direct correlation. Those who show profits at a level above 8 percent make no bones about *not knowing it all.* They hire help or have staff men available who can the solve the problems of equipment selection, personnel placement, wage negotiations, legal matters such as pension plans or whatever and, *above all*, the crucial element of taxes.

Begin a year-end tax planning session with your CPA or tax specialist. Do it *before* year end. There are related decisions that must be made now, decisions that cannot wait until April 14. Time spent asking advice now will pay off not only now but in the years to come.

We have devoted some time to the singular subject of depreciation and cash flow. We have seen profit leader firms who have one major piece of equipment with *two kinds* of *depreciation* on their tax schedules—some parts of the press at straight life, some later additions at the double declining balance method. They have listened to sound tax advice. Here they are at better than 10-percent net profit and making and keeping money on less sales than the average. Almost without exception *they plan ahead*, be it for sales and marketing or for finance and taxes.

Taxes are serious business. We have a lot of wars to pay for. Let's let the non-planner and non-tax strategist pay for them. Let's use every legal tool available for full and complete tax avoidance where at all possible.

Time and space prohibit a full tax calendar being published here. But the fact that the dates take up *nine full pages* in the 1974 Commerce Clearing House Tax Guide ought to tell you something about the need to get with it.

Chapter 26
Ratios as an Aid
to Sales Management

"It was a common saying. . . . . that men ought not to
investigate things from words, but words from things;
for that things are not made for the sake of words,
but words for things."

—Diogenes, 200 AD

Victor N. Stein, chairman of the financial committee of Printing Industries of America, and leading that group of executives responsible for the Ratio studies, said this in the 1975 Ratio study foreword: "We firmly believe effective use of the Ratios is related to the improvement in industry profits this year."

To this we say amen! This past year has been one of recovery, more solid than I had even hoped for. Instead of the normal one-in-five firms being a Profit Leader, the new proportion is one-in-four! That's really indicative of extra effort in top management effectiveness in: (a) getting proper levels of productivity, (b) pricing the product properly, and (c) servicing respective markets satisfactorily.

When we examine these Ratio "Road Maps to Profit Land" we find all kinds of uses for them. Exhibit 1 shows us the case of a printer who will be reaching for $2 million in sales this year. He has set his sights on that market size, with normal growth patterns and with the same relative cost patterns that he had the past year when he was a 5.3 percent net profit printer. He has set as a standard for his operation the total cost structure of a same-size firm, but this year run as Profit Leaders operate. They end up with almost 12 percent net. This is the goal he has set for the year.

Exhibit 1 shows our firm and the Profit Leader. And that's just the beginning point. What do we do with the variances? It is very easy to let this Exhibit 1 be the end rather than the beginning. And really, if we want a better ending, this has to be the beginning point. Let's take the third column of data and break down any variance from the target standard.

This leads us to Exhibit 2. Here we have shown each of the eight items of cost variance that we must "manage" in order to get to our goal of 12 percent net. Less than 40 percent of our total problem is in the "Direct Cost" area of either Labor or Direct Factory Wages and Fringes! Better than 33 percent in General Factory Overhead and another 28 percent in General Office or Sales Overhead. These last two areas total better than 61 percent of the areas where profits can be improved.

These last six general classifications are some $30,400 greater than the combined Labor and Materials variance. That's 60 percent more than the dollars we could improve in those first two basic elements of our production cost! Yet these, because of their very nature, are often more difficult to pinpoint and to correct. The reason is that they are usually the areas where management attention is needed. If we are marginal printers, such attention is a must for survival. It we are fairly good in profits, we have a tendency toward passing them over lightly. Not so, if we are Profit Leaders. That is what separates the two.

Exhibit 1
The Sample Firm and The Profit Leader

	Profit Leader Budget	Our Budget	Variance from P/L Budget (worse)
Sales value of product	$2,000,000	$2,000,000	
Materials used:			
Paper	499,600	483,600	$ 16,000
Outside purchases & other ...	253,600	277,600	(24,000)
Total material	753,200	761,200	(8,000)
Factory payroll	525,600	587,600	(62,000)
Factory expenses:			
Fixed	99,200	108,200	(9,000)
Variable	86,400	102,400	(16,000)
Total factory expenses	185,600	210,600	(25,000)
Total factory cost	1,464,400	1,559,400	(95,000)
Gross profit	535,600	440,600	(95,000)
Administrative cost	138,800	155,200	(16,400)
Selling expenses	162,800	170,200	(7,400)
Total G & A and sales cost	301,600	325,400	(23,800)
Operating income (deficit) ...	234,000	115,200	(118,800)
Net other income and (expense) .	5,000	(8,200)	(13,200)
Net profit (deficit) before taxes	239,000	107,700	(132,000)

Now just what can the Ratio Study do for a management man, other than the owner-operator? Or other than the "numbers man," the treasurer or controller? Let's take Sales Costs. While our example in Exhibits 1 and 2 shows Sales Costs to be the nearest in line to our standard, or the area where we could make the *least* gains, let's not leap to conclusions.

At this time let's get away from the individual account classifications and take an overview of the situation. Most sales vice presidents are not usually the men who pore over the bits and pieces of the Ratio Studies. It is usually the task of the president or the treasurer and the controller. They are the Number Men. But this isn't right! Other operational department managers can get as much from the Ratio Study.

Here's an example: Exhibit 3 lists the items of interest to the sales vice president of any size firm. Here is what is available to him as guide posts toward better Sales Cost control, better salesman productivity. That's often *more important* than the number of sheets off the two-color 38" press! What are the salesman's expenses in relation to sales dollars he has produced? This and many more questions are covered in the Ratio Studies if we make the effort to find and use them.

Exhibit 2
Budget Improvement Areas, Our Firm Vs. Standard
(Basis: 1976 Sales Effort of $2 million)

	Variances in Total Budget	
Areas for Management Vigilance	*Dollars*	*Percent*
Direct cost area:		
Material cost	8,000	6.06
Direct factory labor	42,800	32.42
Total direct costs	50,800	38.48
Indirect cost areas: or overhead		
Factory indirect labor and supervision	19,200	14.54
Factory fixed costs	9,000	6.82
Variable factory costs	16,000	12.12
Total factory overhead	44,200	33.48
Front office overhead		
Administration costs	16,400	12.42
Sales costs	7,400	5.62
Financial income/expenses	13,200	10.00
Total office overhead	37,000	28.04
Total indirect costs (overhead)	81,200	61.52
Total variance from standard	132,000	100.00

Exhibit 3
Sales and Marketing References:
PIA 1975 Ratio Study, Part 1 and 2

Sales or Marketing Cost and Economic Data   *Number of References*

1. Operating cost data
    Total departmental selling costs. 54
2. Details of selling costs 245
3. Sales value of production
    Per employee, with and without executive, productivity
    of sales effort 383
4. Departmental payroll data
    To evaluate cost of selling, individual averages as well as totals . . 192
5. Employee data (sales personnel). 115
6. Value-added basis of sales costs
    By total department and detail costs. 222
7. Balance sheet data
    Relationships of sales to total assets, net worth, etc. 20
8. Profit on sales
    True markup determinations by sales size, process of
    manufacturing and prime product classifications 99
9. Capital expenditures related to sales and market
    response with related equipment expansion areas. 176
    Total sales and marketing data decision helpers available 1,506
Part 1: 36 pages; Part 2: 44 pages

Our listing in Exhibit 3 is only from Parts 1 and 2 of the five-part Ratio Study series. What a wealth of gold is waiting to be mined by the men who seek to improve the firm's position!

Probably someone will say: "There's only $7400 Sales Cost variance from standard" and would conclude that is very little to worry about. But our purpose is not to use this one example as an answer to all things. Take instead the situation of a larger firm, with sales in several high cost market areas. Fig. 1 poses some gems you could know as fact:

In Fig. 1 we've taken the Sales Cost on three firms of equal size, $2 million in Sales. Compensation is for salesmen, without sales executives goofing up our averages. Compensation equals salary and commissions plus taxes and fringes. Sales per salesman begins to point out the relationship of sales effort or productivity.

This is just a beginning point on the long, hard road toward profit improvement. We just had a call from a company owner who has six 38" presses of various configuration. He is doing a very big piece of business in his state, yet he doesn't have a handle on overhead cost control. Sure, he is making money, but he wants to make more! His is to be congratulated on recognizing the not-so-obvious fact that additional profit dollars are within his firm already if he can locate them and control them as they should be located and can be controlled.

Not everyone is willing to get into the fight to do that. Perhaps that's why there are so few Profit Leaders. It has always been that way.

Fig. 1
Sales Costs and Productivity
(with regional variances)

Metro Region	Sales Cost ($)	Compensation ($)	Sales per Salesman ($)
New York	181,000	23,000	507,000
Chicago	157,000	33,000	389,000
Dallas	196,000	21,000	249,000

Chapter 27
Profit Leaders and
Press Selection

"The decision will depend
on a judgment or intuition
more subtile than any
articulate major premise."
—Justice Oliver Wendell Holmes Jr.

Much of the basic economics of printing profitability is related directly to press productivity and operating cost. Because of this one fact, press selection, be it for new uses and new markets or simply replacement purposes, is a most critical decision point for owner/managers of printing plants.

There are a few basic steps the profit leaders take before they decide which press to acquire. Now of course, all of them do not follow them precisely. Yet at some time or other, each of the well managed firms we know goes through basic decision-making steps.

First: Most profit leader firms have an overall long term plan or corporate strategy for growth and profitability. These long term goals are usually set at the Board of Director and/or Presidential levels, with added support from the various staff and line operating department heads. These are usually broad directives concentrating on marketing areas and end products with some consideration given to personnel and equipment (plant) needs. These long-term adopted policies then need the maximum follow-up efforts of the line and staff members of the management team.

Second: Within the framework of the operating management team must be the ability to recognize the *impending obsolescence* of equipment. This is done by the profit leaders *before* it becomes a matter of fact. They watch and prepare for it. This part of total corporate life is, in most firms, a major responsibility of the triumvirate made up of the plant manager, the head of sales/marketing and the controller/treasurer. If their titles differ as we cross company lines their areas of responsibility do not. They are usually production plus sales plus finance. The first sign of obsolescence is not necessarily recognized by any one of these three executives. It most likely will be passed up the line by a pressroom foreman, a sharp pressman, a salesman or a cost accountant! But the major point of fact here is that it has *to be watched, recognized* and *evaluated* before equipment failures through obsolescence shrink profits and lose customers!

Third: This is perhaps the most difficult to describe properly. For want of a better term I shall label it "awareness of press capabilities." This has to do with press designs, specifications, production speeds and all other related matters including *initial cost* and *operating costs.* All these hinge upon the simple questions: Will this press give me a *superior competitive position* in my area and/or product field? Will this particular press give my sales personnel the advantage in service, or quality, or cost? If it doesn't do it at least in one of those basic three *why even consider it?* Move on to better things.

Fourth: Having now considered the specific press needed for the maximization of productive and marketing support to the long-term policies (number one of this series) then comes the matter of consideration for a new press or a used press. At this point, we are not seriously considering different equipment manufacturers; this has been determined at point number three. We are now at the final stage of equipment selection. New or used. And why!

Fifth: The final step is to determine the method of acquisition. Do we buy, or do we lease? A very cold, hard case can be made for either choice. It is again a matter of finances, cash flow, cash availability, long term "fixed cost" relationships, etc.

So there it is in essential simplicity.

1. Long-term corporate strategy for growth.
2. Vigilance to recognize impending obsolescence.
3. Press awareness of capabilities and competitive advantage.
4. New *vs.* used considerations.
5. Financial considerations (economics of ownership and operation).

Perhaps a few comments are in order at this point.

To begin with, the size of the firm doesn't have very much to do with the final choice of ways and means. We can often see better results from smaller well-established firms that are both growth- and profit-minded. They know what they are doing.

If it were size alone that accounted for soundness in management decision-making then these firms would not have made the recent headlines they have: Penn Central, Rolls Royce, Lockheed, Pan Am, Ling Temco Vaught, General Dynamics, Chrysler, A & P and the list grows and grows. Now we can add W.T. Grant and others. . . . who will it be next month? If size were the factor, all of these firms would have had the proper long term strategy, the correct operational planning, the right way to plan for profits, control overall costs, establish firm and sound cost controls. But for the most part, these huge firms fell flat on the old kisser. A nose dive in front of everybody.

If memory serves correctly, more than one seminar and more than one graphic arts meeting has had a man on the podium extolling the virtues of profitability. . . while he sat at the helm of a 3 percent net firm! Some of the various regional and national trade associations have been a party to this in times past. There are even articles on the subject, written as if size in printing equates high levels of profit and ultra sound decisions. Bah, Humbug! Some profit printers laugh at this hypocrisy!

Who is to tell the industry what? In reality no one. Each firm has to go it alone. Oh to be sure, we measure ourselves by the "peer group" for averages, for a "handle on costs," etc. But when it comes down to what is right for us, not the printers in New York, or Chicago, or even "cross town" will determine it. What is right for us in our own peculiar circumstances? Very few really get at the right answers.

There are some old wives' tales such as "Getting the right answers just 51 percent of the time will put you in the winner's circle." What a bunch of ripe rotten baloney! For what if in the quest for right answers a printer makes only four of five misjudgments. Yet, suppose each one is related to the single point of press selection! How very stupid! Yet we all go through life following such nice little rules of thumb, or are they rules of dumb?

In our Exhibit 1, we have shown what happened to some 871 printers in 1974 as revealed in the 1975 PIA Ratio Studies. One doesn't have to be a top grade statistician to see that we have a real whipsaw effect all along the line. Each group of "other" printers or marginal firms is passed in total dollar income by the profit leaders of the next lower size group. Now this is no recent phenomenon, but one we have been observing with great regularity since about 1966! It has grown stronger as one of the more critical indicators of differentials between good and "so-so" management. These profit dollar returns tell a real story!

There is no way of knowing how often the right press selection in 1966 affected profits in 1970! Or how choice decisions in 1976 will translate themselves into profit dollars in 1978! We have no data collecting evidence of that sort. Oh, to be sure we have had efforts like the McKinsey Report to PIA in 1966 on the subject of "Targeting the Printer's Marketing Approach to Higher Profits." And a good one it was too. It still is, in point of fact, a good report. The principles contained within it have not changed. Another one like it was the McLagan Report on "Planning a Profitable Balance Between Equipment & Sales." Just as good in 1976 as when it was presented to PIA in 1968. Both these reports were outgrowths of the Harris-Intertype report of 1963. That particular effort zeroed in on these four special decision points facing the printer:

1. How does management respond to market change?
2. What is the corporate cost/price discipline?
3. Is there a coordination of equipment and sales?
4. As the business grows, does the skill required to manage grow as well?

PIA has had one special report on all four subjects. Yet the overpowering annual report of profit leaders *vs.* the "others" group doesn't change much. Twenty to 25 percent are leaders, the rest are still following far behind, profit-wise. For some are not so wise about profits!

Volume is not the answer. Give me a 3 percent profit printer at $2.6 million in sales and 99 times out of 100, he'll still be a 3 percent profit man when sales reach $3.2 million! Volume alone is not the answer.

Exhibit 1

How 871 Firms Produced Profit Dollars in 1974

Size Class	Average Firms in Even $1,000's		Sales Value of Production
	Income Average		
	Dollars	Percent	
10 Giant Profit Leaders	$2,420,000	10.75%	$22,500,000
18 Large Firm Profit L.	961,000	13.02%	7,383,000
28 Other Giant Firms	775,000	4.01%	19,339,000
62 Medium-large Profit L.	321,000	11.21%	2,863,000
44 Other Large Firms	211,000	3.17%	6,664,000
72 Medium Profit Leaders	110,000	11.85%	928,000
190 Other Medium-large	88,000	3.27%	2,688,000
37 Small Profit Leaders	46,000	12.20%	377,000
231 Other Medium Firms	29,000	3.09%	940,000
21 Very Small Profit Leaders	19,000	12.10%	157,000
103 Other Small Firms	16,000	4.28%	374,000
55 Other Very Small Firms[1]	nil	—0—	171,000
871 Total Firms			

Notes: 1. An almost perfect case of Break-even. How tragic!
Source: Absolute Data Section of 1975 PIA Ratio Study Part 1.

One thing seems to stand out. This comes by observation and not from statistical data. Those in the past who made the right market decisions, press selection-wise, personnel choice, and price policy were the profit leaders in 1966, and in 1974 and again in 1976, the great American 200th Birthday Year. I guess even Old Ben would agree to that. That wise old fella said once concerning a certain Mr. Bradford, another Philadelphia printer, and then postmaster: "I thought so meanly of him for it, that, when I afterward came into his situation, I took care never to imitate it." Such were his comments upon a rival's unfair business practices.

But we're not talking of unfair practices. We are speaking of current changes in presses, of decisions to meet market competition, and of operating costs we have to live with. Don't imitate the "other" local printers in choice of presses. If everyone else has a two-color 38" press, *that in itself* is reason enough to consider another size! In cases like this, perhaps a small web has a ready market awaiting it. But only investigation can tell you this.

And what about productive capacity? A few weeks ago we sat at supper with a PIA printer and his regional trade association executive. The association's production services manager was along as well. When new presses became the subject of discussion, the production services manager and I mentioned the same manufacturer's name. Was our friend going to investigate these new imports with 15,000 i.p.h. rated speed? Perhaps it won't suit his market or needs, but then again it just might be what he is looking for in a new press.

But because he is well on the road to profit leadership and aggressive growth, I feel sure *he'll investigate fully* before the final decision. Then his decision in 1976 most surely will affect 1977 profits.

Old Ben also said, "Time is money." And 15,000 i.p.h. sure beats 10,000 i.p.h. By some 50 percent. That's where the old cost relationships need to be put to the test. The final grades come out on the bottom line. And here's hoping you have high passing marks!

Chapter 28
Overhead Differentials

"Overhead or burden costs are usually spread
over the work in process on the basis of
departmental or machine-hour rates—founded on
a more or less detailed study of operating
conditions—or in proportion to direct labor costs,
labor hours, or total direct labor and material cost."

—W.A. Paton
Accountant's Handbook

About ten years before the shots were flying around parts of New England at the birth of this country, Old Ben the printer from Philadelphia had reissued his classic. . . Poor Richard Improved! The time was 1765 and the comment that so aptly fit this effort seems to be "But there are two nobler virtues, industry and frugality, which tend more to increase wealth, power and grandeur of the community, than all the others without them." Of course we are not investigating community affairs here, but those of printers . . . but from the overall view of logic, you are almost forced to the same conclusion. Along the lines of "Keep thy shop and thy shop will keep thee!"

If it seems we are overly caught up in the internal affairs of production costs and other types of total operating costs for printers it is because they make up a goodly part of this game we call industry, and that is with or without the frugality mentioned above! Going over a fairly long computer run of costs for both sheetfed and web presses we noted the basic differences between various size printing firms and between printers who have a different end product. These differences occur even when there are conditions wherein the basic costs of a direct nature are 100 percent identical. While 100 percent identical is redundant, we use it to produce an effect . . . we hope!

Many articles over the years have tried to show the reasons for variations in pricing a product. We just received in the mail a sample of such a price problem to be used at a seminar.

You know the kind I am referring to . . . where everyone at a seminar or workshop prices out a job or series of jobs and they compare end results during one of the class sessions. It is an ideal way to get everyone involved in the subject matter by total participation. We all use it: PIA, NAPL, regional associations and even those of us who are brave enough to venture forth on our own. But here is the nut, the gist, the point of it all: even if every participant had identical equipment with an identical direct labor cost, even within the same union scale structure, almost without exception costs would be different! And if most printers sold by cost plus markup for profit (not value selling) then because costs vary, the resulting prices for the same job would of necessity vary as well.

That is as absolute as most things, surpassed only by Mr. Franklin's assurance for us of death and taxes. It is that absolute! To show this, we have taken three identical sheetfed presses, name and/or type and style are not of interest here. Only the internal cost structure when similar units are compared by firm size. All three firms are in the same union, all capitalized the cost center with the same previous year cost dollars, all use the same method of tax write off for depreciation dollars. But there all similarity ends. Well, almost all similarity!

The three firm sizes used in our examples are the small printer under $500,000 sales volume, the mid-size firm with about $800,000 in sales volume and the medium-large firm with sales of $2,000,000 and up. In the development of these cost figures we have used the internal cost structure of a three-year running average of profit leader firms (better than 8 percent net) in these size groups.

Within these three cost structures we've limited ourselves to examining the basic areas of what most of us consider when we use the term "overhead." These five areas are:

1. Finances and payroll taxes on direct labor.
2. Indirect labor, plant supervision and related fringes and payroll taxes.
3. Other fixed factory costs.
4. Variable factory expenses: the supplies, repairs and maintenance items of a general nature.
5. The combined amounts for general administration costs and selling expenses.

One big factor to note is that four of the five are out in the plant. But they are strong in numbers only! For if we consider Dollars of cost, what accrued and is accruing on the office side of the door to the plant is of the *far greater weight* and effect on profit! And it is this singular point that perhaps sinks more ships enroute to the Profit Islands in the sky than any other single cause. Most printers are not aware of overhead in office and sales areas that *must be recovered* by the pricing process. 'Tis a fact of life.

Take the small press in Exhibit 1. The four plant overhead costs for the small firm total $8,299.84 while the front office and sales overhead is $9,478.66, a dollar differential of $1,178.84 or 14 percent MORE than all the plant overhead! In the medium size firm the differential dollars are $1,212.44 and represent 12.8 percent of total plant overhead. When we get into the larger plants the cost relationships change . ˙. for the better. The weight of front office and sales costs *drops* to a bit below those of plant overhead totals. With the large firm the dollar differential is $1,623.20 with this being 16 percent under plant overhead!

Exhibit 1

Small size one color press capitalized at $12,000.00
Union scale lithographer at $7.20 per hr. 35 hr. week, 10
holidays, 4 weeks vacation. Overhead allocations per group
size Profit Leadership in three size ranges:

	Small Firm	Medium Firm	Medium/Large Firm
Base Sales Value of Production	$400,000	$800,000	$2,000,000 plus
ONE SHIFT			
Direct labor—str. time	$11,592.00	$11,592.00	$11,592.00
Fringes & payroll taxes	2,645.50	2,787.02	3,184.07
Ind. labor & supervision	2,228.17	3,044.04	3,317.23
Total factory labor	16,465.67	17,423.06	18,093.30
Depreciation	1,200.00	1,200.00	1,200.00
Other fixed factory costs	1,116.00	912.00	912.00
Variable factory costs	2,310.15	2,729.05	2,719.63
Total factory cost	21,091.82	22,264.11	22,924.93
G & A and sales costs	9,478.66	10,684.55	8,509.73
Total cost	$30,570.48	$32,948.66	$31,434.66

Budgeted hourly costs				
Factory cost only	80%	$ 16.38	$ 17.29	$ 17.80
	70%	18.72	19.76	20.34
	60%	21.83	23.05	23.73
Total cost at	80%	23.73	25.58	24.41
	70%	27.13	29.24	27.89
	60%	31.65	34.11	32.54

The net effect of this is the obvious conclusion that the medium size firms are not as cost control minded as the smaller plants or their bigger brothers! That may or may not be true.

What many of us do is overlook not only the effect of overhead, but the fact that it is only a means to an end. Note in our three Exhibits it is always the mid-size printer with the highest total dollar cost at this particular press cost center. There is even a $5,100 dollar differential between mid-size cost and large firm cost for the multi-color $100,000 press. But here's the final bit of news concerning these firms. In the final measurement point— net Operating Profit—the mid-size firms average 11.72 percent while the small are at 11.35 percent and the larger fellas at 10.97 percent.

This is because hourly costs are only one-fourth of the overall basic economic formula that gets to the year end P & L.

1. Material input cost usage (two parts to this one).
2. Hourly cost of operation (plant and office combined).
3. Levels of productivity (a real bucket of worms).
4. Pricing policy.

During the past these have been wrapped up in such terms as cost/price discipline with the stress upon numbers two and four above. But they are further affected by numbers one and three.

To get to such a cost series as this, which is what we usually use in either book format or in client reports, we use a formula that is more than a bit complicated. It consists of some 28 input and/or calculations for first shift costs and at least 72 when doing first and second shift work. Considering the one shift only these are made up of the following:

9 input data facts (if it is a one man press crew)
6 internal program controls within the basic formula usually stored within the computer in some form or fashion.
13 various mathematical functions, add plus multiply plus divide, etc. . . as programmed.

I have had quite a bit of interest expressed by firms that have been into estimating by computer as to how to program costing into either computers for such determinations as monthly updated hourly costs, or the methods to do it by old-fashioned pencil and calculator. The system is the same, the formula basically the same, only the mental requirements are different!

If we prepared work sheets for web press costs, following this same formula, we would find results exactly like that in our previous examples and exhibits. For the problem is still one of men, machines and materials. Press configurations don't change results at all. The principles don't change, only the size of the numbers.

Exhibit 2

Medium size one color press, Capitalized at $30,000.00
Union Scale Lithographer at $8.25 per hour, 35 hr. week, 10
Holidays, 4 weeks vacation. Overhead allocations per group
size Profit Leadership in three size ranges:

		Small Firm	Medium Firm	Medium/Large Firm
Base Sales Value of Production		*$400,000*	*$800,000*	*$2,000,000 plus*
ONE SHIFT				
Direct labor—str. time		$13,282.50	$13,282.50	$13,282.50
Fringes & payroll taxes		3,031.30	3,193.46	3,648.41
Ind. labor & supervision		2,553.11	3,487.96	3,800.99
Total factory labor		18,866.91	19,963.92	20,731.90
Depreciation		3,000.00	3,000.00	3,000.00
Other fixed factory costs		2,790.00	2,280.00	2,280.00
Variable factory costs		3,032.80	3,526.58	3,501.20
Total factory cost		27,689.71	28,770.50	29,513.10
G & A and sales costs		12,443.76	13,806.96	10,955.26
Total cost		$40,133.47	$42,577.46	$40,468.36
Budgeted hourly costs				
Factory cost only	80%	$ 21.50	$ 22.34	$ 22.91
	70%	24.57	25.53	26.19
	60%	28.66	29.78	30.55
Total cost at	80%	31.16	33.06	31.42
	70%	35.61	37.78	35.91
	60%	41.55	44.08	41.89

For a Western Gear Web doesn't cost the same when running business forms as it does when doing label work or commercial printing. Each type of firm has a completely different overhead cost structure.

We have included here two additional exhibits. Exhibit 2 shows the same conditions with a larger single color press capitalized at $30,000. Exhibit 3 is a multi-color press of $100,000 cost. The same variations exist in these cases to a lesser or greater degree.

Exhibit 4 shows how this same principle carries through when comparisons are made that are a bit more specific. In this example we've taken an upstate New York printer and compared his cost of operating three different units of phototypesetting equipment as compared to a national trade typesetter who is representative of the profit leader group in typesetting. In these conditions we have imposed like labor cost and like depreciation. This makes total direct labor input equal and the first part of factory fixed cost equal.

Major areas of differential in overhead occur at these points:
1. Supervision and indirect labor cost: the 391 dollar difference equals better than 32 percent of the trade shop costs!

Exhibit 3

Larger size multicolor press, Capitalized at $100,000.00 with a crew of two Lithographers, Union Scale combined rate $16.30 per hr. 35 hr. week, 10 holidays, 4 weeks vacation. Overhead allocations per group size Profit Leadership in three size ranges:

	Small Firm	Medium Firm	Medium/Large Firm
Base Sales Value of Production	$400,000	$800,000	$2,000,000 plus
ONE SHIFT			
Direct labor—str. time	$26,243.00	$26,243.00	$26,243.00
Fringes & payroll taxes	5,989.11	6,309.50	7,208.38
Ind. labor & supervision	5,044.33	6,891.36	7,509.83
Total factory labor	37,276.44	39,443.86	40,961.21
Depreciation	10,000.00	10,000.00	10,000.00
Other fixed factory costs	9,300.00	7,600.00	7,600.00
Variable factory costs	6,958.90	7,969.03	7,882.34
Total factory cost	63,535.34	65,012.89	66,443.55
G & A and sales costs	28,552.78	31,199.69	24,663.85
Total cost	$92,088.12	$96,212.58	$91,107.40

		Small Firm	Medium Firm	Medium/Large Firm
Budgeted hourly costs				
Factory cost only	80%	$ 49.33	$ 50.48	$ 51.59
	70%	56.38	57.69	58.96
	60%	65.77	67.30	68.78
Total cost at	80%	71.50	74.70	70.7⊥
	70%	81.71	85.37	80.84
	60%	95.33	99.60	94.31

Exhibit 4

Client Firm: An Upstate N.Y. Printer vs. Nat'l
  Trade Typesetter P.L.

Department: Typesetting

Three profit centers: #1 Singer Keyboard

#2 Compuscan OCR Page Reader 172;

  # Comp. ACM 9000

Hours @80% 1,383   70% 1,210.125 60% 1037.25

Factors .0007230   .0008263   .0009640

Std. Work Week   37.5 hrs.

Annual Hours   1950

Vac + Holiday 221.25

Net Annual Hours 1728.75

Budgeted Hourly Costs per Your Financial Statements

Cost Centers	Albany #1	#2	#3	Nat'l Trade Shop #1	#2	#3
Direct Labor Str. Time	7,485			7,485		
Fringes & P.R. Taxes	1,975			1,975		
Total Direct Labor	9,460			9,460		
Supervision & Indirect L.	1,587			1,196		
Total Factory P.R.	11,047	11,047	11,047	10,656	10,656	10,656
Fixed Factory Cost Depreciation & Rentals	270	5,500	1,995	270	5,500	1,995
Other Fixed Costs	228	4,649	1,686	173	3,516	1,275
Sub-Total L + F/C	498	10,149	3,681	443	9,016	3,270
Variable Exp. Supplies etc.	1,621	2,976	2,068	1,619	2,870	2,032
Total Expenses	2,119	13,125	5,749	2,062	11,886	5,302
Total Factory Cost	13,166	24,172	16,796	12,718	22,542	15,958
General Administrative Selling Expenses Total G & A & Sales	4,825	8,859	6,156	4,675	8,286	5,866
TOTAL COST	17,991	33,031	22,952	17,393	30,828	21,824
Hourly Rates on Total Cost @ 80% Prod.	13.01	23.88	16.59	12.58	22.29	15.78
@ 70%	14.87	27.29	18.97	14.37	25.47	18.03
@ 60%	17.34	31.84	22.13	16.77	29.72	21.04

2. The same 32 percent differential stays with the cost of other fixed factory overhead. Take the scanner, the dollar variance between the two is $1,133 . . . still 32 percent which is coincidental.
3. There's only a 7 percent differential at the administration and sales cost level and almost none at the factory supplies level.

Total cost differential on the scanner is about 7 percent or $2,203.

And this is the biggest reason prices vary as they do. And they always will.

The same principles hold true for CRT, VDT, OCR, and even saddle-binders and mailing label machines! And it will never be any different. Not even if all print shops were nationalized.

Chapter 29
The Risk-Takers
Lean Toward Marketing

"Your doubts are the private detectives
employed by dislike to
make a case against change or choice."
—W.R. Rogers

The old Chinese proverb states: "Great risk brings great rewards." This is not from our present generation Chairman but from some great philosopher of many centuries ago. How true it is. We have seen case after case where men in positions of decision making have held back from taking the risk and wonder why they do not grow or prosper. On the other hand we've seen some who stick out their necks and weather the storm to find themselves up on plateaus of glorious sunshine and a more profitable tomorrow.

Recently we had the opportunity of working with a corporation wherein we had the advantage of data comparisons of common ownership but with different plants and executives responsible for growth and profits. For the sake of this chapter let us say that it is the ABC Corporation with two plants within the same general marketing area, same union conditions, same opportunity for equipment selection and product marketing. Each plant is about twenty to thirty years old. But within the past six years each has left the old patterns and gone on to new heights of growth. But these heights are not at all alike.

Perhaps something can be learned regarding growth and what some call the "levels or plateaus of growth." It is different with every firm. Some level off at $300,000 and $600,000 and then again at $900,000. Others will level off at $500,000 and $1,000,000 and again at $2,000,000. Still others will not level off at all, but will have an almost straight line of growth. Most people seem to favor this latter kind of growth pattern as it appears to be the most "stable   But is it really?

We were once in the office of a company president far removed from the example firm in this chapter. He had just gone through a very dramatic expansion, new big press, new big camera, new big multi-pocket gatherer-stitcher-trimmer, new photocomp unit, new building, new lease, new this and new that. And a whole bunch of new fixed cost to deal with in the upcoming '76 budget. His break-even point for '76 far exceeds his total sales value of production for '75. But with the good old American Risk Taking Spirit, he thinks he'll do it this year . . . and better.

To make matters worse he is in what many of our readers would call an "economically depressed area" with little or no total capital goods expansion expected in that region for the years 1976–1978. Other printers in his area are pulling them in close to the chest just as if they were in a poker game and had a pat hand of four kings with ace high! He is what is known in the trade as a risk taker. His company has grown to be about number 20 or 25 in his state . . . but just about three years ago it was number 87 or 118! In about three years we expect to see him as number 7 or 8 in the state!

Being pushed for better time for management and marketing he was at the point of decision: do I or do I not hire another estimator to take the load off my back, or do I get a small stand-alone computer to do my estimating for the firm? His decision was the latter.

Here's what he evaluated: "The estimator will need break-in time. He will still need much of my time in reviewing his work. My time is best spent before customers . . . selling our productive effort. Our salesmen will benefit from another full-time estimator. But if we get a small in-house computer to run the numbers on the estimates, I will be relieved of much time, my salespeople will get faster and give better, more accurate service. My basis of cost control now has one more strong link in it. Our 'image' to the customers would be better, they will get accurate estimates faster."

All things considered he could not have come to any other conclusion in his particular set of circumstances. Within a few weeks of our discussion he placed the order for the computer. It is now earning its way.

The actions of this aggressive company president are like the long-term management men who run plant X in our example.

Plant X management has had a long series of expansion decisions this past decade. They seem to come about every other year. One year it was a big bindery move, next it was a new big two-color press, then this past year it has been a four-unit small web press to complement the sheetfed operation. After each year of expansion, the company consolidates its position in the market place. Rapid growth is therefore on an every-other-year basis. The profit figures also have a sort of saw-tooth effect, climbing high *every other year* (not following general national economic trends at all!) being high in the *years following* the equipment expansion. If you'll note our Exhibit I you'll see plant X as the top line of the dual comparison. Expansion years were '72 and '74 and '76.

The years for dramatic sales growth have been '73 and '75 and will be '77! He has planned on it. The score card to date shows that this long-term capital expansion/marketing growth can be controlled, can be maintained if you know *where you are* and where you are going and most importantly, *HOW* you are going to get there.

This isn't something that can be canned like a budgeted hourly cost study and packaged neatly up for guideline purposes. It usually comes by long, hard hours of study, of the agony of heart-tearing decisions and then having the guts to put those decisions into action. At that point most management men have to take their banker into their trust and then they had better know whereof they speak.

Plant Y is representative of far more of our present day printing firms who play a close to the vest position of ultra conservatism. They are all out for the long-term straight line growth. Plant Y in this corporate body has management men who are really close balance sheet watchers. But not acclimated to risk taking. In the broadest sense of the word, Y is craft oriented. X is leaning towards marketing. Both are serviced by the same major equipment firms. One has a lot of small one-color presses and all kinds of itty bitty bindery gadgets . . . the other now has several two-color presses and a new four-color small web.

At the beginning of the Seventies they were only $120,000 apart in sales dollars, now they stand at $575,000 differential and that will most likely move up to close to a full million by 1977.

Now in all this talk of sales growth, we are often guilty of overlooking the effect of inflation upon our corporate well being. Our Exhibit II should be useful to the firm that wants to do some serious long-range forecasting and growth planning. The overall growth of plant X during the five years under review was $1,100,000. That is very good! But when we take into account inflation it becomes a much lower figure. Still good by all means but not what it first appeared to be! Better than 35 percent of plant X expansion dollars were just pass-through dollars taken up with inflation. Valueless as far as adding one bit to our firm's solid growth and well being.

Worse than that, plant Y had some 40 percent of their growth dollars offset by valueless inflation. Because of this monster, each firm had one year of total dollar growth with an actual non-inflationary sales decline or *setback*!

Exhibit I.

X Plant: Capital Expansion Years
1971, 1973, 1975

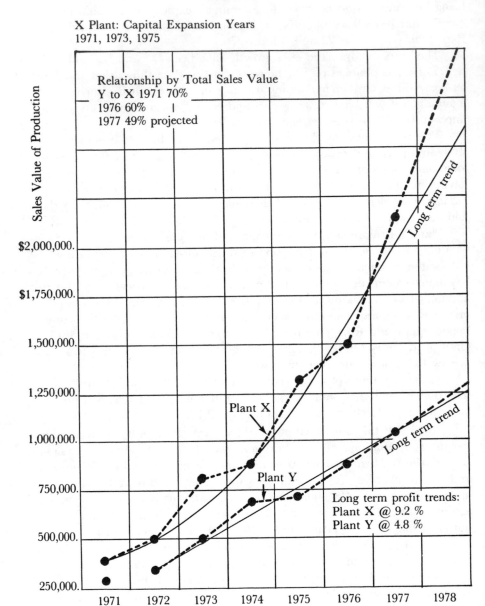

Exhibit II
ABC Corporation with Plants X & Y
Comparative Growth Data

Plant X	1971	1972	1973	1974	1975	1976	Base Totals
Sales Value of Production	$400,000	$500,000	$800,000	$875,000	$1,300,000	$1,500,000	$5,375,000
$ Growth over Previous yr.		100,000	300,000	75,000	425,000	200,000	1,100,000
Less Inflation		40,000	50,000	80,000	87,500	130,000	387,500
Actual Growth		$ 60,000	$250,000	$(5,000)	$ 337,500	$ 70,000	$ 712,500
Plant Y							
Sales Value of Production	$280,000	$350,000	$500,000	$675,000	$ 725,000	$ 900,000	$3,430,000
$ Growth over previous year		70,000	150,000	175,000	50,000	175,000	620,000
Less Inflation		28,000	35,000	50,000	67,500	72,500	253,000
Actual Growth		$ 42,000	$115,000	$125,000	$(17,500)	$ 102,500	$ 367,000

For purposes of example 10% inflation is assumed for these base period years.
All figures rounded to nearest even $500 amounts.

Actual Growth after Inflation:

Plant X	15%	50%	(.6%)	39%	5%	40%
Plant Y	15%	33%	25%	(2.6%)	14%	15%

Long term trend of growth: X @ about 24 to 25%; Y at about 14 to 15%.

Just as a note for minor recognition: during this period plant X contributed some $320,000 profit dollars to the overall corporate kitty while plant Y had a share some *two hundred thousand less*! As the old man said: "Great risk brings great rewards." You can not survive, let alone expand, without a certain amount of risk. It has ever been that way. The gutsy ones prevail and are usually well up among the profit leaders. That's even true with wild cat oil wells! Be they in Texas or Alaska or Arabia! It's an economic fact of life and bankruptcy court.

Exhibit III.

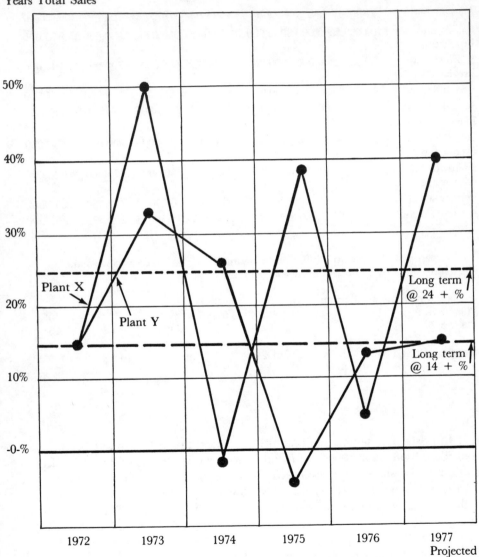

Growth Percentage
Sales Value of Previous
Years Total Sales

DATE DUE